A CHILD'S INTRODUCTION TO

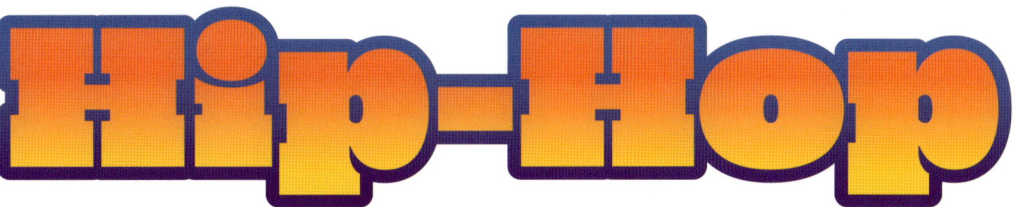

A CHILD'S INTRODUCTION TO

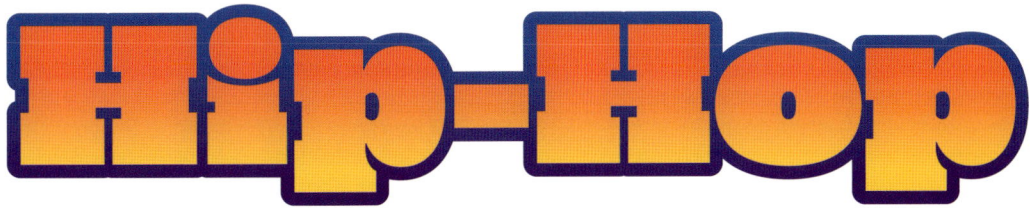

Hip-Hop

The Beats, Rhymes, and Roots of a Musical Revolution

JORDANNAH ELIZABETH

ILLUSTRATED BY
MARKIA JENAI

BLACK DOG
& LEVENTHAL
PUBLISHERS
NEW YORK

Black Dog & Leventhal Publishers
Hachette Book Group
1290 Avenue of the Americas
New York, NY 10104
www.hachettebookgroup.com
www.blackdogandleventhal.com

First Edition: August 2023

Black Dog & Leventhal Publishers is an imprint of Perseus Books, LLC, a subsidiary of Hachette Book Group, Inc. The Black Dog & Leventhal Publishers name and logo are trademarks of Hachette Book Group, Inc.

The publisher is not responsible for websites (or their content) that are not owned by the publisher.

Black Dog & Leventhal books may be purchased in bulk for business, educational, or promotional use. For more information, please contact your local bookseller or the Hachette Book Group Special Markets Department at Special.Markets@hbgusa.com.

The Hachette Speakers Bureau provides a wide range of authors for speaking events. To find out more, go to www.HachetteSpeakersBureau.com or email HachetteSpeakers@hbgusa.com.

Print book interior design by Katie Benezra

Graphic illustrations courtesy of Getty Images: pages 12, 19, 20, 21 by ulimi; pages 7, 8, 10, 17, 22, 29, 40, 52, 58, 60, 66, 74, 88, 90, 92 by Zoonar RF; pages 8, 10, 17, 22, 40, 52, 60, 74 by OliaFedorovsky; and by amovitania (throughout)

Library of Congress Cataloging-in-Publication Data
Names: Elizabeth, Jordannah, author. | Jenai, Markia, illustrator.
Title: A child's introduction to hip-hop : the beats, rhymes, and roots of a musical revolution / Jordannah Elizabeth ; illustrated by Markia Jenai.
Description: First edition. | New York : Black Dog & Leventhal, 2023. | Includes bibliographical references and index. | Audience: Ages 8–12 | Summary: "With A Child's Introduction to Hip-Hop, parents can teach their kids about their favorite musical genre through this beautifully illustrated exploration of the history and origins of hip-hop, beginning with the 'Holy Trinity' of DJ Kool Herc, Afrika Bambaataa, and Grandmaster Flash, to today's Kanye West, Cardi B, and more, all leading up to the 50th anniversary of the birth of hip-hop in August 2023" —Provided by publisher.
Identifiers: LCCN 2022023130 (print) | LCCN 2022023131 (ebook) | ISBN 9780762481026 (hardcover) | ISBN 9780762481033 (ebook)
Subjects: LCSH: Rap (Music)—History and criticism—Juvenile literature. | Hip-hop—History—Juvenile literature.
Classification: LCC ML3531 .E45 2023 (print) | LCC ML3531 (ebook) | DDC 781.64/9—dc23/eng/20220516
LC record available at https://lccn.loc.gov/2022023130
LC ebook record available at https://lccn.loc.gov/2022023131

ISBNs: 978-0-7624-8102-6 (hardcover); 978-0-7624-8103-3 (ebook)

Printed in China

APS

10 9 8 7 6 5 4 3 2 1

For Greg Tate

The Grandfather of Hip-Hop Journalism — J. E.

For my Mama, Ebony Laird,

who kept the music and art alive in me — M. J.

Contents

Introduction

When you hear the words "**hip-hop**" or "rap" music, you probably have an idea in your head of what the music sounds like or you think of your favorite songs you've heard on the radio or streaming online. We now live in a world where hip-hop is everywhere, and everyone has an idea of what it is. But did you know hip-hop has a long and interesting history?

In this book, we are going to explore the history of hip-hop from the very first days it was created in the South Bronx in New York City in the 1970s right up to the 2020s.

Hip-hop is a style of music that connects electronic **beats** and **samples** of prerecorded music with words. The people who perform this music are called **rappers**. Rappers have a gift of using **rhyme** and storytelling set to music to make listeners understand the way they look at the world and what they experience.

THE ROOTS OF HIP-HOP

For centuries, African American and Black people created music from their imaginations, creating beats and rhythms with their mouths and singing melodies if there weren't instruments that were readily available. Enslaved Black people all over the United States sang old hymns called "Black spirituals" while they were forced to labor against their will. This music grew into "work songs" that were sung to the drum-sounding rhythm of workers banging railroad ties into the ground so trains could travel on them.

Spirituals and work songs helped Black workers and enslaved peoples express the sadness they were feeling. They used instruments like banjos and guitars to put these songs to music. Some people started to write new songs and lyrics that could be played for audiences. Lyrics are the words in a song. These musicians began traveling to entertain people in small clubs around the American South. This music was eventually called "the blues."

Blues music became very popular in the 1920s because of singers and musicians like Bessie Smith, Robert Johnson, B.B. King, and many other artists. They made soulful music about life and its struggles. The hip-hop and **rap** music we listen to today is closely related to the blues and to other kinds of music like jazz and rock.

How Hip-Hop Began

THE BRONX, NEW YORK CITY

The very first days of hip-hop culture began in the early 1970s in the Bronx, New York.

The Bronx is a borough (or section) of New York City that was home to many African Americans and Latinx Americans who sometimes saw poverty and violence in their communities. Not all people of color are poor, but for many poor youth, music and art helped them express their unique views of the world.

▲ The Whitestone Bridge connects the Bronx neighborhoods of Throggs Neck and Ferry Point Park.

BLOCK PARTIES

THERE WERE A lot of block parties in the Bronx in the 1970s. Block parties are outside events, usually held in cities where neighbors and community members come together and put on a big party in the middle of the street! Block parties tend to be for people of all ages and they are all about community.

Hip-hop culture began at these block parties. New types of music were played and new dance moves were created. These young people were inventors. Their way of life was so lively and powerful that hip-hop music and its culture spread everywhere.

EARLY FASHION

ALONG WITH THE fun of block parties, hip-hop culture has had a lot to do with fashion and style. Over the years, hip-hop style has changed a lot, but items like gold or diamond jewelry have stayed the same since the very beginning. Hip-hop style is tied to Black and Latinx street style. Kids would wear comfortable clothes they could dance and run in. Fashion designers like Tommy Hilfiger began to make clothes for the hip-hop culture and the style grew more popular. Later on, rappers like Def Jam's Russell Simmons, Sean Combs, and many others began creating their own fashion lines.

▶ A Bronx block party in the 1970s

THE ELEMENTS OF EARLY HIP-HOP CULTURE

HIP-HOP CULTURE HAS FOUR KEY ELEMENTS:

- DJing or turntabling
- MCing
- Graffiti art
- Break dancing

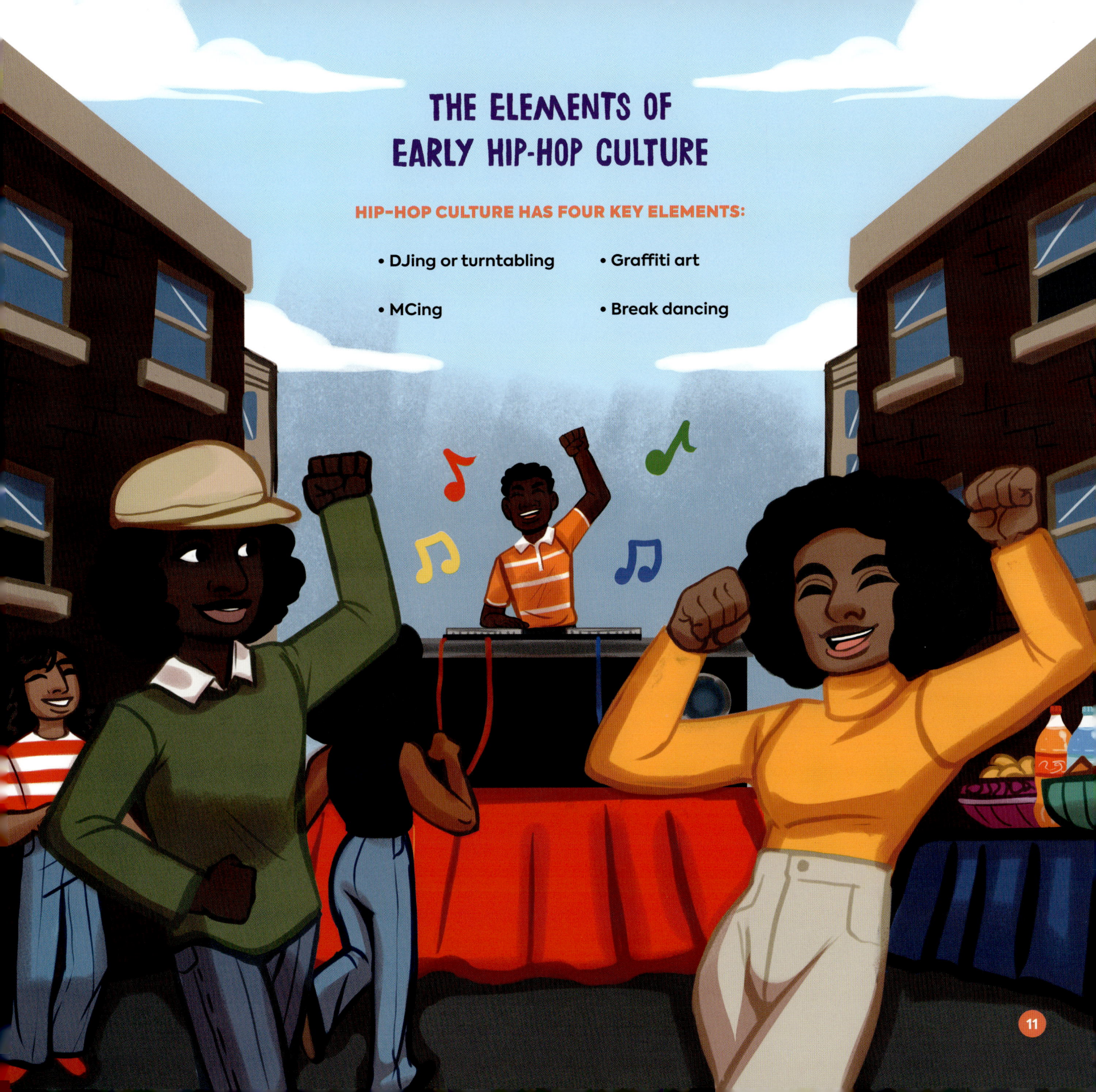

DJING OR TURNTABLING

A LOT OF the music played at block parties was by artists called **DJs**. You've probably seen a DJ before. They turn or spin dance music on records on turntables (record players). Not only did the DJs choose the music that would be played to entertain the partygoers, but they also had microphones and spoke to the crowd and got them excited!

DJ Clive "Kool Herc" Campbell was known to be one of the best DJs around because in 1973, at his sister Cindy's back-to-school party he took DJing and turntabling to new heights.

Kool Herc found a way to make the percussion sound, which is the drum sound, of a song stand out by using two record players and a mixer. He could make the beat of a song longer by switching back and forth between the two records, playing it over and over. This created a whole new type of music and a way to keep people excited and dancing. This type of DJing was called **breakbeat**.

Kool Herc's style became the foundation of the hip-hop sound. Even today, beats are essential to the way a rapper performs their rhymes and the mood and pace of the song.

▶ DJ Kool Herc

MCING

MCING, ALSO KNOWN an "emceeing" or "rapping," is another essential element of hip-hop. MC comes from the term "master of ceremonies," which was a title given to a person who hosted parties and dance events. Originally, **MC**s would entertain the partygoers by making them laugh and getting the crowd excited with the latest dance craze or fast-paced music.

Over time, MCs began to turn their humor, charm, and talent for language into rhymes or "raps." They would speak to the rhythm of the music and create clever sayings; many times their raps would be improvised, meaning they didn't write anything down or memorize what they were going to say. This form or rapping later became known as **freestyling**. MCs would create raps that described the energy of the crowd and would boast and brag about how cool and talented they were.

MCs became so good at rapping about how great they were, they would compete with other rappers. They would challenge them to show the crowd who was the best rapper based on how original the rapper's rhymes were, how well they could embarrass the rapper they were competing against, and how excited the group would get.

At the end of each rap battle, the crowd would choose who was the best rapper by cheering the loudest for their favorite rapper.

▲ A rap battle

GRAFFITI ART

GRAFFITI IS THE visual art side of hip-hop. Starting in the 1970s, the youth of the Bronx and New York City began "tagging" their names inside and outside subway trains, subway stations, and on the sides of buildings. It all started after "TAKI 183" from 183rd Street in Washington Heights began writing his nickname around his neighborhood in the late 1960s. At first, no one knew who he was and the city became fascinated by this mysterious "writer" whose name seemed to be everywhere. In 1971, he finally shared that his name was Demetrios in an interview with a newspaper.

Young people realized that they too could become famous for their graffiti. Tagging and graffiti soon became a part of the hip-hop culture. They started using brightly colored spray paints to stand out.

Later in the 1970s graffiti culture became even more organized and stylized. A new competition called the "style wars" started. The pieces got bigger and young writers began to sketch their work in notebooks before painting them. Young writers would get together for "writers' benches" and study each other's sketches before painting them. Older writers would take young graffiti artists under their wings and teach them all that they had learned. Even though the art was competitive, it also created a tight community of artists. This community still lives on today. Graffiti is now global and lives on as new generations of artists continue to paint large-scale and small-scale tags.

Graffiti Activity

GRAFFITI IS A fun form of art that can be done anywhere: on a wall, on a bedroom door, on the side of a train. You can make a graffiti mural all on your own! Here are some steps to help you make some cool hip-hop–based art:

1. You can sketch your graffiti image on a piece of paper.

2. Most times, graffiti is written as a "tag" of the "writer" or artist's name. You can choose your own graffiti name. Be creative!

3. Once you've chosen your letters, word, or tag you can sketch your idea with a pencil or ballpoint pen.

4. The words should pop off the page. You can make this happen by outlining a bubble around the flat words and color in the surrounding bubble.

5. You can shade in the letters or the surrounding bubble with your pen or pencil.

6. Once you have your graffiti tag sketched and looking just the way you like it, grab another sheet of paper and make the same sketch with colored pencils or markers.

7. When your colored graffiti tag is complete, you can ask your parents if you can put a larger mural on your wall. It's okay if you can't! From now on, you'll know how to make graffiti! When you get older you'll be able to tag on a larger scale.

Even though graffiti has traveled all over the world, it also still isn't accepted everywhere. Many people think graffiti is a crime since graffiti artists sometimes paint buildings and subways without permission. Because of this, many artists have to hide who they really are with nicknames.

Graffiti is risky but this doesn't mean it isn't an important part of hip-hop culture. It helped young artists of color find their passion and express creative talent. They turned something negative and illegal into a positive community-building phenomenon that has a rightful place in hip-hop history.

BREAK DANCING

BREAK DANCING IS another important element of hip-hop. The phrase **break dancing** comes from DJ Kool Herc's breakbeat type of DJing. Dancers learned to use the long drumbeats to perform a dance style that used moves from gymnastics and martial arts, pushing dancers to flip, split, and spin on their heads!

Young people also used fast footwork and humorous moves to grab the crowd and attract attention. Break-dancers became known as "B-boys" and "B-girls" and during many of Kool Herc's parties he would set aside time for the dancers to show off their footwork by yelling "B-boys, go down!"

Like all the elements of hip-hop, there was a competitive side to the break dancing. Young people would gather around in a big circle to give the dancers plenty of room to do backflips and complicated twirls. Each dancer would show their skills.

Break dancing has a number of different dance steps. A few of these are freezes, toprocks, downrocks, and powermoves. The combination of these movements along with a dancer's own unique twists to the style created a widespread craze across the Bronx and New York City's Black and Latinx communities. Break dancing is still alive and well today. Dancers continue to create new moves and give partygoers and audiences amazing shows! There are also dance competitions all over the world that embrace break dancing.

▲ People break dancing downrock moves

The Birth of Mainstream Hip-Hop

(1979-1982)

SUGAR HILL RECORDS

In the early and mid-1970s hip-hop culture was going strong in Black and Latinx communities, spreading from its birthplace in the Bronx to all over New York City and beyond. The music, rapping, clothing styles, dances, language, and parties were quickly becoming popular and it seemed like people couldn't get enough of this new way of life.

Music **producer** Sylvia Robinson saw the potential of hip-hop and started a **record label** called Sugar Hill Records with her husband and fellow producer, Joe Robinson. Sugar Hill Records was named after Sugar Hill, a neighborhood in Harlem, just a few miles south of the Bronx in the borough of Manhattan. Countless Black jazz greats, poets and writers, artists and dancers have lived and worked in Harlem since the 1930s, so it made sense that the first known hip-hop label would be named after this incredible neighborhood and Black arts community.

▲ Sylvia Robinson

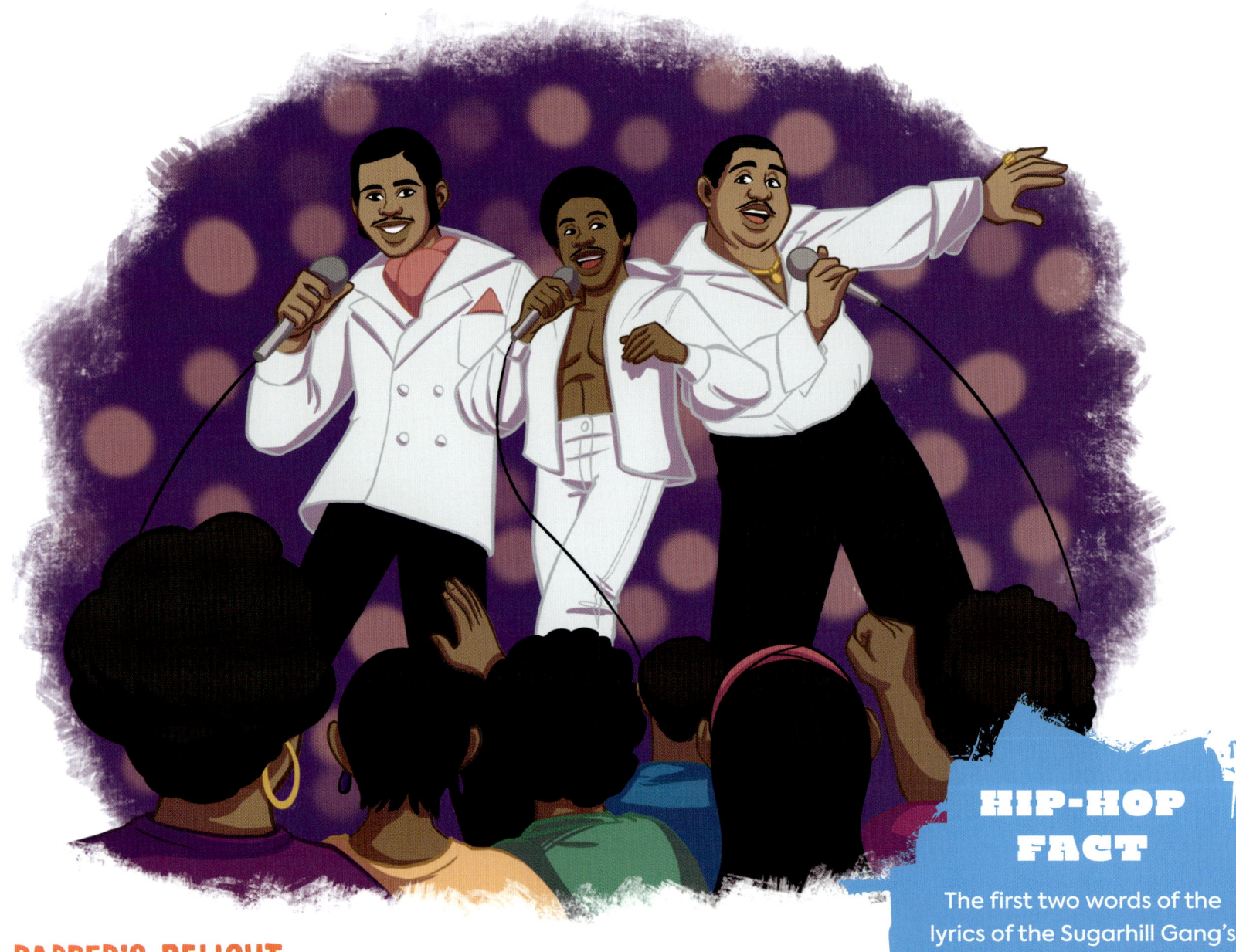

HIP-HOP FACT

The first two words of the lyrics of the Sugarhill Gang's "Rapper's Delight" are "hip-hop"!

RAPPER'S DELIGHT

SYLVIA DIDN'T JUST name her record label after Sugar Hill, she also set out to form a hip-hop group by the same name. She searched for the right performers and met Henry "Big Bank Hank" Jackson, Guy "Master Gee" O'Brien, and Michael "Wonder Mike" Wright. These three MCs had the right style, attitude, and charisma she was looking for and she named them the Sugarhill Gang.

The Sugarhill Gang recorded the fun and catchy song "Rapper's Delight" and, in 1979, the song hit the radio airwaves and swiftly took the world and mainstream music by storm.

"Rapper's Delight" sold over one million records and was the very first successful rap song in history.

▲ The Sugarhill Gang

GRANDMASTER FLASH & THE FURIOUS FIVE

SYLVIA ROBINSON MADE hip-hop a household name but members of the hip-hop community who came before the Sugarhill Gang didn't take her hit record seriously. Sylvia didn't give up.

She looked for more artists in rap. In 1982 she scored another hit with Grandmaster Flash & the Furious Five's powerful and visionary rap song

▲ Grandmaster Flash & the Furious Five

HIP-HOP FACT

In 1980, the popular white disco, post-punk band Blondie released their own version of a rap song called "Rapture" where the group's lead singer, Debbie Harry, tries her hand at MCing. For the song's music video, Blondie invited rapper Fab 5 Freddy and graffiti artists Lee Quiñones and Jean-Michel Basquiat to make appearances. This is an example of the connection of white rock artists and Black hip-hop culture leaders, creating a "rap rock" tradition that would live on into the next century.

"The Message." Even though this song was very successful Sylvia had to convince Grandmaster Flash & the Furious Five to perform a song that gave a clear and honest account of what was going on the Black community. She wanted the group to tell the story of life in the inner city and show the world the reality of poverty and violence in the Black community. When the group finally decided to record the song, they had to trust Sylvia who eventually turned out to be right, and the world got the first-of-its-kind story of Black life in the United States through the poetry and rhymes of rap.

Many people think that "The Message" is a very powerful piece of rap music in hip-hop history. It has inspired generations of rappers and still does today. "The Message" later became the very first hip-hop song to be archived in the Library of Congress, a place where important American historical items are saved and documented for the world to learn about.

HIP-HOP FACT

Another influential song that came out in the early 1980s was Kurtis Blow's "The Breaks." Blow was the first rapper to sign a contract with a major record label, helping him achieve widespread success. The Treacherous Three's 1980 song "The New Rap Language" was an influential song that came from a pioneering hip-hop group who formed in 1978.

AFRIKA BAMBAATAA AND THE SOUL SONIC FORCE

AFRIKA BAMBAATAA IS one of the most unique electronic artists in hip-hop history. He is known for his interesting use of samples. Samples are pieces of songs mixed together with drumbeats and other melodies. Afrika used samples from the German rock group Kraftwerk and their songs "Trans-Europe Express" and "Numbers." His song "Planet Rock" went on to international success being played in numerous countries all over the world.

▲ Afrika Bambaataa and the Soul Sonic Force

Afrika committed his life and work to exposing young people and the Black community to the Universal Zulu Nation. He was inspired by the 1964 British film *Zulu* about the rebellion of the Zulu people against the British. He admired how connected and loyal the African tribe was, and his name came from that of the Zulu chief, Bhambatha. Afrika created a hip-hop–based community of dancers and DJs. He was the first hip-hop performer to travel overseas.

Afrika Bambaataa had a huge impact on the culture and will forever be known as one of the early leaders of hip-hop.

THE NEW YORK CITY RAP TOUR

THERE WERE HIP-HOP artists who were very cultured and interested in art. Because they were interested in European art and culture, hip-hop artists knew that Europe would love what they were doing in New York. They wanted to share and expand the music to places they admired and wanted to travel to.

Rapper, artist, and filmmaker Fab 5 Freddy and music promoter Kool Lady Blue connected with the Europe 1 radio station and French-based record labels Disc'AZ and Celluloid put together the first cross-cultural hip-hop tour called The New York City Rap Tour. The aim for this musical tour was to expose French music lovers to the fresh new hip-hop sound of the United States. London also got a taste of hip-hop as the tour made two stops in the British city. Afrika Bambaataa was a part of this tour along with many DJs and artists include PHASE 2, Grand Mixer D.ST and the Infinity Rappers, the Rock Steady Crew, and more.

HIP-HOP'S NEXT STEPS

MEANWHILE IN NEW YORK CITY, hip-hop continued to grow alongside the white rock scene. Music clubs began to play new wave, punk, and hip-hop music alongside one another in popular night clubs like the Roxy.

▲ The New York City Rap Tour

Hip-Hop's New School Era

(1983-1984)

NEW SCHOOL HIP-HOP

Hip-hop and rap kept growing in 1983 and 1984. Hollywood began to tell the stories of hip-hop in South Bronx, rappers were selling millions of albums, and hip-hop fashion and language were spreading all over the world. Some people were writing stories saying that hip-hop was a "fad," or a short-lived cultural phenomenon, that would disappear as fast as it had arrived.

Little did they know that in 1983, a new era of hip-hop was getting started and would push hip-hop into its rightful place in popular mainstream music and culture. This new sound and style of hip-hop was called "new school" hip-hop.

While old school hip-hop was made up of sounds that borrowed from the funk and disco music of the 1970s, new school hip-hop music's sound was inspired by drum-machines and rock music. The new school's lyrics were more aggressive, and the attitude of b-boys and -girls became more serious.

RUN-DMC

THE HIP-HOP group Run-DMC was formed in Hollis, Queens, New York, in 1983 by members Jason Mizell, Joseph Simmons, and Darryl McDaniels.

Joseph Simmons was introduced to the hip-hop world by his older brother Russell who was already a part of New York's hip-hop scene. Joseph didn't just receive an amazing real-life education in hip-hop from his brother, he was also offered a life-changing job: DJing for the popular rapper Kurtis Blow. Russell was Kurtis Blow's manager.

Joseph worked closely with Kurtis Blow under the stage name "DJ Run, Son of Kurtis Blow." He eventually became popular enough in the hip-hop world to create something of his own. After releasing an unsuccessful **single** "Street Kid" Joseph didn't give up. He knew his talent could go further and decided to form a rap group, using part of his DJ name "Run" to create Run-DMC with his longtime friend Darryl McDaniels (DMC) and a DJ they'd admired since they were young, Jason Mizell (Jam Master Jay).

It took some convincing to get Russell to assist his little brother again, but Russell agreed to help

them record a new song and find a record label to support their careers.

In 1983, Run-DMC's first single, "It's Like That/Sucker MCs," connected with hip-hop and rap fans and did well on the R&B *Billboard* charts. The song's bold sound and powerful lyrics were fresh and attractive to music fans.

Another important contribution Run-DMC made to hip-hop was their street style–inspired fashion. The rappers and DJs of the old school era wore glamorous, colorful clothes like shiny sequined shirts and tight flamboyant pants and shoes. Run-DMC dressed more closely to break-dancers and the style of clothes kids were wearing on the street during that time. They wore Adidas tracksuits and unlaced shell-top shoes, Kangol hats and leather jackets, rejecting too much color and almost wearing their clothes like supercool uniforms.

▲ Run-DMC (Jason Mizell, Joseph Simmons, and Darryl McDaniels)

Hip-Hop and Film

IN THE EARLY 1980s, four hip-hop–inspired films were shared with the world.

Wild Style is considered to be the first hip-hop film in history. The movie came out in 1983 and includes appearances from some of the most influential rappers and artists of the time such as ZEPHYR, Fab 5 Freddy, the Cold Crush Brothers, the Rock Steady Crew, Grandmaster Flash, and others. *Wild Style* follows the adventures of a graffiti artist living in the Bronx whose work and competitive nature attract a journalist who connects hip-hop art culture with the upscale art world of downtown Manhattan in New York City.

In 1984 there were two films released about break dancing culture and the lives of DJs and break-dancers in the Bronx called *Breakin'* and *Beat Street*.

Krush Groove is a movie that came out in 1985. It is a music-based comedy that follows the story of the early days of the iconic hip-hop record label Def Jam Recordings.

These films defined hip-hop culture even more, connecting with an audience who had never been to the Bronx or New York City with the dance, art, drama, fashion, and style of the newly growing hip-hop culture.

LL COOL J

AROUND THE SAME time in 1984, a sixteen-year-old rapper named James Todd Smith from Bay Shore on the south side of Long Island, New York, came onto the hip-hop scene. LL Cool J, as he was known, was a good-looking, forceful, and charming young rapper who had been working on his rap style since he was a young boy.

Like Joseph Simmons, LL's family worked hard to help him realize his dreams of becoming a rapper. His family bought him the equipment he needed to produce and record his own music. Between the ages of ten and sixteen, LL focused on creating and producing a sound and rap style that was like no one else.

He used the equipment he was gifted to record demo songs by himself. When he felt they were good enough, LL sent the songs to as many record labels as he possibly could. One of the record labels he sent his music to was Def Jam Recordings, an up-and-coming label run by Russell Simmons and Rick Rubin.

Rick Rubin received LL's demo and liked it very much. Def Jam Recordings offered the young rapper a record deal and together they released the label's very first official piece of music, LL's single "I Need a Beat" in 1984.

"I Need a Beat" went on to sell ten thousand copies, giving LL Cool J the success he needed

to prove he was a great rapper and helping Def Jam grow as a business. They received a distribution deal from a major record label called Columbia Records. Columbia helped Def Jam reach more listeners and press more albums, and in 1985 LL Cool J's first full album, *Radio,* was released to the world.

LL's rapping was very clever and unique. On *Radio* he showed his talent by including elements of storytelling, insults, and disses to others in the rap world, and bragging about himself in ways that were funny and believable. LL was wise

beyond his years. His rapping wasn't childish or silly. He was serious and confident. The **album** revealed strength and clear, cool lyrics that helped bring hip-hop and rap to the next level of professionalism and power.

Radio sold five hundred thousand copies five months after its release, which was a major success for hip-hop at the time. Over time, the album went on to sell one million copies, making LL Cool J one of the most popular and visible rappers in the world.

▲ James Todd Smith, aka LL Cool J

HERE ARE SOME other popular recordings from the new school era:

1983

Rammellzee and K-Rob
"Beat Bop"

Grandmaster Flash & Melle Mel
"White Lines (Don't Don't Do It)"

The Treacherous Three
"Action"

B Beat Girls
"Jungle Swing"

Grandmaster Caz & Chris Stein (of Blondie)
"Wild Style Theme Rap 1" and "Wild Style Theme Rap 2"

The Rocksteady Crew
"(Hey You) The Rock Steady Crew"

1984

Whodini
"Freaks Come Out at Night,"
"Grandmaster Dee's Haunted Scratch," "Friends,"
"Five Minutes of Funk," and
"Escape (I Need a Break)"

Fat Boys
"Jail House Rap"

T La Rock & Jazzy Jay
"It's Yours"

Art of Noise
"Beat Box"

Grandmaster Melle Mel & the Furious Five
"Beat Street" and "Internationally Known"

1985

Marley Marl
"Marley Marl Scratch"

Doug E. Fresh & the Get Fresh Crew
"The Show" and "La Di Da Di"

Schoolly D
"P.S.K. What Does It Mean?" and "Gucci Time"

Roxanne Shanté
"Bite This"

MC Shy D
"Rapp Will Never Die"

BEASTIE BOYS

IN 1984, DEF Jam Recordings released the humorous and outlandish single "Rock Hard" from hip-hop trio Beastie Boys. Beastie Boys had been a group since 1981, but "Rock Hard" helped bring them into the hip-hop music sphere. The song included heavy rock and roll guitar riffs. Beastie Boys, who are white and Jewish, were able to take the connection between the hip-hop and rock world and pack them into heavy, in-your-face songs. Beastie Boys' 1986 album, *Licensed to Ill,* was the first hip-hop album to become number one on the *Billboard* charts.

In 1986, Beastie Boys joined the Raising Hell Tour with Run-DMC, LL Cool J, and the hip-hop group Whodini. Fans were excited to see these leaders of hip-hop's new school share a stage.

The amazing success of Run-DMC, LL Cool J, and Beastie Boys during the new school era helped push rap and hip-hop forward into what is now known as a "golden age." Hip-hop and rap became more advanced, more political, more violent, more widespread, and began to be taken more seriously by white Americans in the upper and middle classes.

▲ Beastie Boys (Michael "Mike D" Diamond, Adam "MCA" Yauch, and Adam "Ad-Rock" Horovitz)

Hip-hop Instruments

Amplifier (amp)—used in hip-hop and other kinds of music to increase the sound of the music. It looks like a big speaker.

Microphone—also called a "mic," it played a big part in the early hip-hop culture. DJs and MCs used microphones to rap and get crowds excited. Microphones are still an important instrument in hip-hop music.

Cable—connects microphones and amps to main musical production boards.

Turntable—a circular plate that rotates to play a record. Turntables have been used since the beginning of the hip-hop era and are important to the sound of the music.

Drum Machine—an electronic drum that creates multiple drum sounds that can all play at once. The Roland TR-808 drum machine, often called an "808," is popular in the hip-hop world.

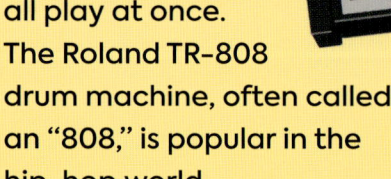

Synthesizer—an instrument that creates sound electronically. They were used a lot in the 1980s to create a modern electronic sound in hip-hop.

The Golden Age of Hip-Hop (1986-1993)

Hip-hop's golden age is one of the largest and most exciting eras of rap and hip-hop. It gave the world a wide range of different styles, sounds, and personalities, more than any other time in hip-hop culture.

MARLEY MARL'S SUPPORT OF THE NEW GENERATION

MARLEY MARL IS a hip-hop producer who got his start as a member of the hip-hop group the Juice Crew. This larger group, also known as a collective, was founded by radio DJ Mr. Magic in 1983 and included musicians like Biz Markie, Big Daddy Kane, MC Shan, Roxanne Shanté, Masta Ace, Tragedy Khadafi, Kool G Rap, and Craig G. Marley Marl got his start as the DJ of Mr. Magic's first-of-its-kind hip-hop show *Rap Attack* on a local New York City radio station.

Marley Marl is known for being a leader in hip-hop's golden age, producing some of the era's most important early albums through his record label, Cold Chillin' Records, which he founded in 1986. He also produced the

▲ Juice Crew

answer record "Sucker DJ's" by Dimples D. as a challenge to Run-DMC's "Sucker M.C.'s" in 1983, as well as the breakout song "Roxanne's Revenge" by fourteen-year-old rapper Roxanne Shanté (see Women in Hip-Hop chapter) in 1984.

Marley Marl also produced a song by the up-and-coming hip-hop duo Eric B. & Rakim. Their 1986 single "Eric B. Is President" is known as one of the first Eric B. & Rakim singles of the early golden age.

ERIC B. AND RAKIM

ERIC BARRIER, BETTER known as Eric B., began his career as a DJ for the local New York City radio station WBLS. This job helped him connect with important people in the local hip-hop community. When Eric B. was ready to start looking for rappers to work with him on a new hip-hop project, he was pointed in the direction of a Long Island, New York, rapper named William Griffin Jr., better known as Rakim.

The duo began writing rhymes and looking for the right songs to sample to create their first recordings. Eric B. went through Rakim's older brother's albums and found a song called "Over Like a Fat Rat" by Fonda Rae from 1982. Eric B. liked the bass line of the song. It was gritty and hard-hitting. But things didn't completely come together until they began to work with Eric B.'s roommate and good friend, the popular DJ and producer Marley Marl.

Marley Marl gave them guidance and support, teaching them the ins and outs of becoming hip-hop recording artists. They gave Marley Marl the records they wanted to use for their first recordings. Though Eric B. has said that Marley Marl wasn't officially their producer because they paid Marley Marl to work the equipment and act as an engineer, Marley Marl is credited with being an important contributor to Eric B. & Rakim's iconic first single, "Eric B. Is President," and its **B side**, "My Melody." The songs were recorded in his home studio and released on Zakia Records in 1986.

"Eric B. Is President" stunned the hip-hop and rap community. Rakim's rhyming style was cool, smart, and laid-back. The song boasted that a Black man and young DJ could run for president and made young rap lovers believe they could do anything.

HIP-HOP FACT

Hip-hop and rap music are known to have a lot of curse words. Some parents have a hard time letting young kids listen to the music because there are often words that kids aren't allowed to say.

▲ Eric Barrier, aka Eric B. and William Griffin Jr., aka Rakim

PAID IN FULL

DEF JAM RECORDINGS cofounder Russell Simmons heard about "Eric B. Is President" and helped the duo get a record deal with Island Records. With the record deal in hand, Eric B. & Rakim began recording their first full album, *Paid in Full,* at Power Play Studios in New York City in early 1987.

The album was recorded in one week as the duo flowed and worked hard to give the world a sensational, laid-back, intelligent hip-hop album. Eric B. & Rakim were right to move so quickly to release their full album because 1987's *Paid in Full* quickly shot to number 8 on the *Billboard* R&B/Top Hip-Hop Albums chart.

Eric B. & Rakim's *Paid in Full* created a new path for future rappers and DJs to follow. Eric B.'s use of several layered samples was a new innovation and Rakim's thoughtful, complex rhymes showed rappers how creative, wise, and intelligent a rapper could really be.

Paid in Full is the album that marked the true beginning and the dawning of hip-hop's golden age, which would take rap and hip-hop to new heights.

BOOGIE DOWN PRODUCTIONS AND KRS-ONE

BOOGIE DOWN PRODUCTIONS, sometimes called BDP, was a gritty hip-hop group from the South Bronx. "Boogie Down" comes from a nickname for the Bronx, the Boogie Down Bronx.

The original members of the group were KRS-One, DJ Scott La Rock, and D-Nice.

They were known in their early career for their rap battles with members of the Juice Crew, Roxanne Shanté, and MC Shan. The rivalry between Boogie Down Productions and Juice Crew was named "The Bridge Wars." The Bronx-based Boogie Down crew thought some of Juice Crew's lyrics said that hip-hop's roots started in Queens, another borough in New York City. BDP didn't like that and released a song called "The Bridge Is Over." The fight between the two rap crews got a lot of attention in the hip-hop community.

Boogie Down Productions released their groundbreaking first album, *Criminal Minded,* in 1987. It was important because it gave very realistic descriptions of life in the South Bronx. The group spoke openly and angrily about the struggles of living with the crime and drugs that plagued the Bronx neighborhood at that time.

Criminal Minded was also important because it planted the seeds of what would later become known as "gangsta rap" and "hard-core rap." Some people thought the album glorified violence and drug use but this was not the direct intention. It was Boogie Down Productions' true reality, and sadly, violence affected the group directly. DJ Scott La Rock was killed in 1987, five months after *Criminal Minded* was released. Their next album, *By All Means Necessary,* moved away from themes of violence in the Bronx and was more political. The name *By All Means Necessary* comes from the famous Malcolm X quote "By any means necessary." Malcolm X was a leader who fought for the civil rights of African Americans.

Rapper KRS-One became more interested in helping to stop the violence in his community. In 1988, he created the Stop the Violence Movement after the death of his friend DJ Scott La Rock was followed by the murder of a young person at a Boogie Down Productions and Public Enemy concert.

The Stop the Violence Movement released a song called "Self Destruction" to talk about how the community needed to make a change and become safer. The song featured lyrics from Boogie Down Productions, Just-Ice, Heavy D, Public Enemy, Doug E. Fresh, MC Lyte, Kool Moe Dee, and Stetsasonic. The Stop the Violence Movement donated the $100,000 that was raised from the release of "Self Destruction" to the National Urban League, an organization that helps city youth find healthy outlets to avoid getting involved in crime, drugs, and violence.

▲ **KRS-One with members of the Stop the Violence Movement**

PUBLIC ENEMY–POLITICAL HIP-HOP TOUCHES THE MASSES

IN 1987 ONE of the most important political hip-hop groups of all time, Public Enemy, was formed. Members Chuck D and Flavor Flav met at Adelphi University in Long Island, New York.

They connected by having similar views about what was going on in the Black community. They worked together to create lyrics that shared their ideas on the health of life in Black America.

▲ **Public Enemy members Chuck D and Flavor Flav**

The rap duo, under their early name "Spectrum City," released a single featuring the songs "Check Out the Radio" and "Lies." During this time, rap battles were happening everywhere. Following the release of the Spectrum City single, Chuck D found himself involved in rap challenges, which led him to release the song "Public Enemy #1" as a response to all the rappers who wanted to battle with him.

Def Jam Recordings cofounder Rick Rubin caught wind of "Public Enemy #1," which was going around the hip-hop scene thanks to Chuck D's connection in the local radio world. This led to a record deal with Def Jam. Chuck D then officially formed the group Public Enemy, which included his friend Flavor Flav and the addition of rapper Professor Griff.

Public Enemy quickly established themselves as a politically charged hip-hop group who were deeply against a new drug that was showing up in New York's lower-income neighborhoods. Their first album, 1987's *Yo! Bum Rush the Show*, gave the world a minimal hip-hop sound along with powerful declarations of political beliefs like the Black nationalist movement.

Their third album, *Fear of a Black Planet*, which was released in 1990, was used as filmmaker Spike Lee's theme song for his important and influential film *Do the Right Thing*. Spike Lee and Public Enemy also released a music video for the same song that found new Black audiences across the United States.

Flavor Flav's Unique Style

FLAVOR FLAV OF Public Enemy had a very different style of dress that matched his comical rap style and lighthearted demeanor.

His signature, or the thing he was known for, was wearing a large clock around his neck.

He also wore colorful clothes and sunglasses.

JUNGLE BROTHERS AND NATIVE TONGUES—THE ROOTS OF SPIRITUAL AND JAZZ HIP-HOP

THE JAZZY, COOL hip-hop group Jungle Brothers burst onto the scene in 1987 with a fresh and breezy sound that was very different from the popular aggressive hip-hop of the day. The group included Mike Gee (Michael Small), Afrika Baby Bam (Nathaniel Hall), and DJ Sammy B (Sammy Burwell). Mike Gee and Afrika Baby Bam were the two lyricists of the group, which means that they wrote the words. DJ Sammy B provided the innovative musical beats. This combination of lyrics and beats helped create an entirely new atmosphere for hip-hop. It was lighter, funny, and more spiritual.

The songs on Jungle Brothers' 1988 album, *Straight Out the Jungle,* were lighter, but still talked about Black pride and they were not as political as Public Enemy. Hip-hop fans found the music refreshing and creative and *Straight Out the Jungle* became a successful album, reaching number 39 on the *Billboard* 200 chart. The group was more Afrocentric and celebratory of Black people, and as Jungle Brothers began to gain success, they connected with other like-minded groups like De La Soul and A Tribe Called Quest.

The music groups Jungle Brothers, De La Soul, and A Tribe Called Quest formed a new hip-hop collective called the Native Tongues.

▲ The Native Tongues

NATIVE TONGUES

THE JUNGLE BROTHERS' success showed that there was a space for different kinds of music and expression in the hip-hop world. But it wasn't until the group heard a young up-and-coming hip-hop trio called De La Soul who opened for them at a show in Boston, Massachusetts, that they realized there were other groups who shared a similar sound and style. The Jungle Brothers felt bonded to De La Soul as if they were kindred spirits who agreed to come together as the first two members of the hip-hop collective Native Tongues.

De La Soul had a fun, happy, and free-spirited hip-hop style. Their 1989 debut album, *3 Feet High and Rising,* spawned a hit song called "Me, Myself and I," which reached number 1 on the R&B/Hip-Hop *Billboard* chart. The song was danceable and fun-loving, and the music video was brightly colored and a little silly.

As Jungle Brothers and De La Soul enjoyed success, they also befriended the too-cool-for-school, bright, and intelligent hip-hop trio A Tribe Called Quest. Tribe members Q-Tip (Kamaal Fareed), Phife Dawg (Malik Taylor), Jarobi White, and DJ Ali Shaheed Muhammad were taken under Jungle Brothers' wings. Q-Tip was first introduced to the world on two Jungle Brothers' songs, "The Promo" and "Black Is Black."

A Tribe Called Quest released a collection of songs that included their popular single "I Left My Wallet in El Segundo" and later "Description of a Fool" before they landed a record deal with Jive Records who released their 1990 debut album, *People's Instinctive Travels and the Paths of*

Create Your Lyrics Like the Native Tongues!

THE NATIVE TONGUES was a fun collective of rappers who were interested in Afrocentric style. Some of the artists like De La Soul and A Tribe Called Quest wrote lyrics that were silly and cool.

Try to write your own lyrics! They can be whatever you like: fun, happy, sad, or serious. Use your creativity and put words together to tell a story!

Rhythm. Fans and music journalists loved the fun, exciting, interesting, and witty album. Their second album, 1991's *The Low End Theory*, was an even bigger success, making it to number 45 on the *Billboard* 200 chart. Their jazzy sound connected with thoughtful, clever, and socially aware lyrics made A Tribe Called Quest an attractive group to a wide range of listeners.

These albums were the seed of a successful and respected music career. They are now considered to be one of the most important hip-hop trios in music history.

THE EXPANSION OF THE NATIVE TONGUES

AS TIME WENT on, the Native Tongues collective grew, adding members Queen Latifah, British rapper Monie Love (see Women in Hip-Hop), and lesser known, but important hip-hop artists and groups of their time: Black Sheep, Chi-Ali, Lucien Revolucien, and Fu-Schnickens. Black Sheep were the first hip-hop group to appear on the popular American late-night talk show *The Tonight Show with Jay Leno,* broadening further and extending the reach of hip-hop.

Other Important Native Tongues Albums

Queen Latifah
All Hail the Queen (1989)

Monie Love
Down to Earth (1990)

Black Sheep
A Wolf in Sheep's Clothing (1991)

▲ Monie Love

The Native Tongues gave the world a different view of Black thought and representation. Their music tore down stereotypes that Black people were violent and sold drugs and instead focused on the beauty, humor, and fun of Black culture and introduced young listeners to bebop and other forms of jazz music.

Women in Hip-Hop

WOMEN IN HIP-HOP MAKE HUGE CONTRIBUTIONS TO THE GENRE

Women have a powerful and important place in hip-hop history. Rap and hip-hop was and still is a male-dominated community. Black women had to work even harder to become part of the community that didn't always accept them. From the earliest days of hip-hop to today, women have contributed amazing music, courageous messages, unique clothing, and much more to the movement.

MC SHA-ROCK— MOTHER OF THE ROCK

MC SHA-ROCK (Sharon Green) is known as the very first woman MC in hip-hop. Growing up in the Bronx, New York, in the 1970s, she entered the very early years of hip-hop culture as a B-girl, break-dancing her way into the hearts and minds of the community. But it wasn't break dancing that made MC Sha-Rock a star and a pioneer of hip-hop, it was her rapping.

MC Sha-Rock is the first woman rapper to record with the otherwise all-male group the Funky 4. Other early members of the Funky 4 were K.K. Rockwell, Keith Caesar, and Rahiem. The group later became the Funky 4 + 1 after Rahiem left the group permanently and MC Sha-Rock left the group for a short time. Their departure brought the addition of MC Jazzy Jeff and Lil' Rodney. When MC Sha-Rock returned to the group, the name was changed to include her as the "plus one."

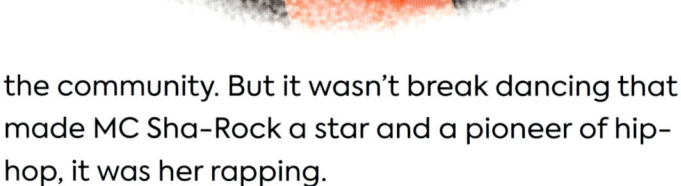

▲ Sharon Green, aka MC Sha-Rock

THE FUNKY 4 + 1

THE FUNKY 4 + 1 were the very first to do many things in hip-hop culture. They were the first mixed gender crew in hip-hop thanks to MC Sha-Rock. They were also one of the only fully formed hip-hop groups in history along with the Fresh 3 M.C.'s and the early formation of Grandmaster Flash & the Furious Five.

The Funky 4 + 1 was also the first hip-hop group that had a microphone for each rapper, which they needed in order to perform dance steps while they performed. They were the first hip-hop group to be on national television after the rock group Blondie invited them to perform on the show *Saturday Night Live* in 1981.

▲ The Funky 4 + 1

In 1979 record producer Joe Robinson was in search of groups who were performing what was then called "talking music" (an early description of rap before it had an official name) in the music industry. He found and signed the Funky 4 + 1, who recorded their first single, "Rappin' and Rocking the House," and in 1981, Sylvia Robinson signed the Funky 4 + 1 to Sugar Hill Records following the success of "Rapper's Delight" by the Sugarhill Gang, releasing "That's the Joint" and "Do You Want to Rock."

The Funky 4 + 1 decided to part ways after their time on Sugar Hill Records but MC Sha-Rock's influence lives on today. She was the very first woman to be seen by national television viewers, letting the world know she was large and in charge, and just as relevant as the men. She was respected by the men around her. Hip-hop pioneer Kurtis Blow said of MC Sha-Rock on the Literary Hub website: "MC Sha-Rock was the most incredible MC! I would put her against any guy during that time. She was just devastating . . . she, to me, was the epitome of a female MC."

Other Early Notable Women Hip-Hop Pioneers (1976-1982)

1. The Mercedes Ladies (Sheri Sher, DJ RD Smiley, Tracy T, Eve-a-Def, Zena-Z, DJ La Spank, and DJ Baby D) were the first all-female rap group founded in 1976.

2. Debbie D was a solo hip-hop artist in the late 1970s and early 1980s.

3. Lisa Lee was the first and only woman to be a member of Afrika Bambaataa & Soulsonic Force who formed in 1980.

4. Sweet and Sour was part of Kool Herc's collective the Herculords.

5. Pebblee-Poo was a member of Master Don & the Death Committee.

6. The Sequence was the first all-female hip-hop group to release a single, 1979's "Funk You Up," a song notable for having the first true hip-hop **hook**. Kurtis Blow's "The Breaks" was inspired by the song.

7. Lady B released her single "To the Beat, Y'all" in 1979.

8. The Winley sisters, Tanya "Sweet Tee" and Paulette, recorded the single "Rhymin' and Rappin'" in 1979, and Tanya released a solo song called "Vicious Rap" in 1980.

▲ Top left: Pebblee-Poo, top right: The Mercedes Ladies, bottom left: Lisa Lee.

MC LYTE

LANA MICHELE MOORER, also known as MC Lyte, got a very early start in her pursuits of a hip-hop career. The Brooklyn native was writing rhymes and songs about the issues facing the Black community in New York City at twelve years old.

She began recording her music at fourteen and by sixteen she had released her profound first single, "I Cram to Understand U (Sam)," in 1987. The song was about a drug that was destroying poor Black communities and tearing apart families. Her intelligence and MC talents got her a record deal with Atlantic Records and by sixteen, she released her debut album, *Lyte as a Rock,* in 1988.

MC Lyte is the first woman MC to release a full solo album. She went on to become the first hip-hop artist (male or female) to perform at New York City's prestigious Carnegie Hall. She was also the first woman to have a gold single (500,000 copies sold) and to receive a solo Grammy nomination for her 1993 single "Ruffneck."

MC Lyte's powerful lyrical style revealed her ability to be clear, assertive, smart, and honest. Her song "I Am a Woman" on her debut album made it clear that it was important for her to share her unique perspective. She didn't want to be "like" the guys; she wanted her point of view and lyrical skills to stand alone and to educate those around her about her own experiences.

Her recording career spanned into the twenty-first century with her 2015 album, *Legend,* creating a legacy and influence that has inspired many that followed her. As a Brooklyn rapper, she opened the doors for lyricists from the borough including Jay Z, the Notorious B.I.G., Lil' Kim, and others. MC Lyte is a true leader and testament to what female-identified people in hip-hop can achieve.

▲ Lana Michele Moorer, aka MC Lyte

SALT-N-PEPA

THE ALL-FEMALE hip-hop group Salt-N-Pepa included Cheryl James, whose rap name is Salt, Sandra Denton, also known as Pepa, and Deidra Roper, DJ Spinderella. Their bright-colored clothes and cool hair styles along with their strong musical skills set them apart from other rap groups.

Before Salt-N-Pepa was officially formed, Cheryl and Sandra recorded a hip-hop song for their friend Hurby Azor who was studying

▲ Salt-N-Pepa (Sandra "Pepa" Denton, Deidra Roper, aka DJ Spinderella, and Cheryl "Salt" James)

recording and music production. Calling themselves Super Nature they decided to record a response to rapper Doug E. Fresh's song "The Show" in 1985. They called their song "The Show Stoppa" and it got some attention after it was played on New York's local radio stations. It made it to number 46 on the R&B/Hip-Hop *Billboard* chart.

"The Show Stoppa" received enough attention to get Salt-N-Pepa a record deal. They quickly went to work recording their first album, *Hot, Cool & Vicious*, which was released in 1986. The album and singles that came from it didn't have much success until producer Cameron Paul made a **remix** version of their song "Push It," which became a huge hit in many countries all over the world.

"Push It" was a catchy and unafraid hip-hop song that was danceable and easy for listeners to enjoy and sing along to. This helped their first album get more popular and *Hot, Cool & Vicious* eventually sold over one million copies, which means the album went platinum. Salt-N-Pepa became the first women hip-hop artists to go platinum.

Salt-N-Pepa have sold over fifteen million albums over the course of their careers and are considered to be one of the most brave, fun, and successful female hip-hop groups in music history.

QUEEN LATIFAH

DANA ELAINE OWENS, better known as Queen Latifah, used the groundwork that previous women MCs had laid for her by infusing her music with a strong feminist and Afrocentric perspective.

Born in Newark, New Jersey, Queen Latifah got her start in the hip-hop world as a **beatboxer** for the music group Ladies Fresh. A beatboxer is someone who uses their voice to make sounds like a drum machine. She knew very early on how important female unity and empowerment were and recorded a demo version of her first single, "Princess of the Posse," which would later become a song on her 1989 debut album, *All Hail the Queen*. Her song got the attention of the influential rapper and television host Fab 5 Freddy and Tommy Boy Records. With a record deal set in place, Queen Latifah would take the world by storm with her innovative, intellectual, feminist lyrics and nods to African history and culture.

Her debut album also spawned one of the most important feminist hip-hop anthems to ever be recorded, "Ladies First," featuring fellow Native Tongues member Monie Love.

"Ladies First" broke through the cultural male-dominated narratives and hypermasculine styles by offering rhymes that praised and celebrated their womanhood and individuality.

Queen Latifah followed up her debut album with *Nature of a Sista'* in 1991 and 1993's *Black Reign*. "Just Another Day . . ." and "U.N.I.T.Y." were two very popular and successful singles, which became her signature songs. It showed her ability to address powerful issues of womanhood with her confident, smooth, and assertive rhymes.

Queen Latifah is considered one of the most successful woman hip-hop musicians of all time. Her declarations of peace, equality, Black beauty, self-esteem, and Black feminist pride gave a generation of girls the strength to love themselves and to never be intimidated by a patriarchal world that would pose challenges for them throughout their lives.

▲ Dana Elaine Owens, aka Queen Latifah

47

Women's Fashion in Hip-Hop

WOMEN IN HIP-HOP had an array of different fashion styles.

Even if they were in jeans and T-shirts, or the West-African dashiki like Queen Latifah, or wearing multicolored clothes and wigs like Lil' Kim and Nicki Minaj, women in hip-hop always expressed themselves in very powerful and unapologetic ways.

▲ Top row: TLC (Tionne "T-Boz" Watkins, Lisa "Left Eye" Lopes, and Rozonda "Chilli" Thomas), Lauryn Hill, Nicki Minaj. Bottom row: Lil Kim, Aaliyah, Missy Elliott.

WOMEN'S UNIQUE STYLES SHAPED HIP-HOP FASHION OF THE FUTURE

There are so many amazing women rap and hip-hop artists who pushed the culture into new territory, breaking up the constant stream of male rappers who dominated the radio, record stores, and television.

Without women like Roxanne Shanté, Queen Latifah, Monie Love, MC Lyte, and others who came before and after them, young women would not feel like they have a voice or place in the culture. These women worked hard to empower others and tell their own stories. They were just as competitive and successful (if not more) than many of their male contemporaries.

Everyone deserves their chance to give their gifts to hip-hop. It's so amazing that there are women who gave strong examples and important rhymes to all who wanted to listen.

LAURYN HILL AND MARY J. BLIGE

THERE ARE SO many remarkable women in hip-hop, but it is important to note two incredible women who merge the lines of R&B and hip-hop, creating a fusion of sound that has inspired the future of both genres.

Known as the "Queen of Hip-Hop Soul," Mary J. Blige began her career in the early 1990s with her debut album, *What's the 411?* One of Sean "Puffy" Combs's first artists on his label, Bad Boy Records, Mary J. had a sound that merged new jack swing,

▲ Mary J. Blige

▲ Lauryn Hill

hip-hop, and soul music. She was featured on early albums from Jay Z and Method Man and was labelmates with the Notorious B.I.G. She wasn't just a singer, she was an icon in the realm of hip-hop from the very beginning and still is to this day.

Her career has spanned over twenty years and inspired a generation of artists. Her foundational sound gave a backdrop to what hip-hop and R&B would become today. Artists like TLC, Mýa, Tweet, Missy Elliott, Ashanti, and many others were able to take the R&B hip-hop sound into the future.

In 1992, a young singer who sat at the center of the hip-hop group the Fugees took the world by storm. At fifteen years old, Lauryn Hill had the voice of an old soul, with a deep alto (lower toned) style that layered perfectly over the Fugees' moody sound.

Her early career with the Fugees anchored her to create her seminal debut album, 1998's *The Miseducation of Lauryn Hill*. The album was largely collaborative, which means many people helped Lauryn make it, but it is important to note and understand that she had a large hand in writing, arranging, and producing the album. Most women are not credited as producers, but Lauryn's ability to create iconic R&B hip-hop songs made her the face of the album's production.

Hill did not release a follow-up album, but she widely toured *Miseducation* on its twenty-fifth anniversary in 2018.

Lauryn Hill and Mary J. Blige are two of the most important R&B hip-hop artists of the twentieth century. Without their music and voices, hip-hop history would not have the foundation to build hip-hop's postmodern sound.

More Notable Women in Hip-Hop

Bahamadia

Foxy Brown

Lil' Kim

Missy Elliott

Trina

Da Brat

Ladybug Mecca

Lady of Rage

Eve

Lisa "Left Eye" Lopes

Jean Grae

Remy Ma

Gangsta Boo

Amil

Rah Digga

Mia X

Yo-Yo

Charli Baltimore

Nicki Minaj

Megan Thee Stallion

Cardi B

Doja Cat

▲ Da Brat

West Coast Hip-Hop

While hip-hop and rap were becoming more aggressive on the East Coast of the United States with albums like Boogie Down Productions' *Criminal Minded* in 1987, a year earlier a young rapper named Ice-T emerged onto the scene on the West Coast.

ICE-T AND WEST COAST GANGSTA RAP

Inspired by Philadelphia-born hip-hop artist Schoolly D, who wrote about gang life in his songs, an ambitious kid going by the name Ice-T decided to try his hand at rapping after graduating from high school in Crenshaw, Los Angeles, and completing a stint in the army. Ice-T showed the intensity of the streets of Los Angeles with the 1986 song "6 in the Mornin.'" His strong storytelling and lyrics about the reality of violence and gang activity were an eye-opening and heavy introduction to what would become West Coast gangsta rap.

After signing a record deal with Sire Records, Ice-T released his debut 1987 album, *Rhyme Pays*, which continued to talk about life on the streets, gun violence, and drugs. The album was very real and music journalists didn't really understand it. But the album successfully reached number 23 on the R&B/Hip-Hop *Billboard* chart. Hip-hop fans heard what Ice-T had to say and they encouraged and accepted the artist's heavy-hitting lyrics and unapologetic rhymes.

But in 1988, an entirely new sound and even darker and violent rap would rise and hit the ears of the American public with the release of the iconic West Coast hip-hop group N.W.A's debut album, *Straight Outta Compton*.

▲ Ice-T

N.W.A AND ICE CUBE'S SOLO DEBUT

N.W.A, WHOSE FOUNDING members included Eazy-E, Dr. Dre, Ice Cube, and Arabian Prince, experienced some success in 1987 with first album, *N.W.A. and the Posse*. But it was their second album from 1988 that really began West Coast gangsta rap. The album's single "F*** tha Police" was a serious call for an end to police brutality, which happened often in Black neighborhoods in Los Angeles.

N.W.A wanted to make it clear that the violent treatment from police toward young Black men was unacceptable and they would not hold back their anger and frustration.

Straight Outta Compton had such an impact on the country when it was released that the police sent a letter to Ruthless Records founder Eazy-E's distribution company to stop putting out the music. Because of this song, N.W.A were never respected by the police. Officers refused to offer them security and protection at their concerts and they were constantly intimidated by the police every time they went on tour.

Unfortunately, N.W.A began to fall apart, and by 1990, founding member Ice Cube had left the group, releasing his debut 1990 album, *AmeriKKKa's Most Wanted*. This was another important album that produced tales of violence on the streets of South Central Los Angeles. Ice Cube's album was created with Public Enemy's musical production team, the Bomb Squad, which

▲ N.W.A

shows the ties between the growth of socially conscious hip-hop and gangsta rap on both coasts at the time. Although Public Enemy was quite different from N.W.A and Ice Cube, all the groups wanted to live in a better world where Black people were not treated differently than white Americans. They were tired of the poverty, lack of jobs, violence, and danger that went on in their communities and they chose different ways of expressing how upset they were by the current state of things.

Ice Cube's second album, *Death Certificate,* released in 1991, continued to challenge racism and unfairness and gave him solid footing as one of the most prominent contributors to the formation of West Coast gangsta rap.

And then in 1991, the world met a new rising star named Tupac Shakur.

TUPAC SHAKUR

TUPAC AMARU SHAKUR is one of the most famous people in hip-hop history.

Tupac was a young poet and artist who attended the Baltimore School for the Arts, where he learned writing and music. He was born in New York City and even named himself MC New York early in his career. But it was after an opportunity came up to make his debut with the well-known Oakland, California, hip-hop group Digital Underground on their 1991 single "Same Song" that would he try out his new rap name, 2Pac. Working with Digital Underground for a few recordings opened the door for Tupac to gain a record deal with Interscope Records and Jive Records.

▲ Tupac Amaru Shakur

His debut album, 1991's *2Pacalypse Now*, dealt with a lot of the same issues that were going on in Los Angeles and the United States at the time, like crime in Black communities, racism, and gun violence. But it was Tupac's personal understanding and poetic lyrics that made him stand out. He had a cadence and style of rapping that had a slight melodic tone, making his voice rise and fall on different words. He had what is called a unique **flow**. The album is said to have been an inspiration to future hip-hop artists like Nas and Eminem.

He would go on to release a few more albums including one of the biggest selling albums in the world, 1996's *All Eyez on Me*. Tupac went through his career, creating his deeply intelligent albums and even acting in movies, but he had a lot of troubles in his personal life. He had been shot but survived. He had been in and out of jail for conflicts and while the world was listening to his music and enjoying his films, they were also watching the pains of his real life unfold on the news on television.

DR. DRE AND HIS DEBUT, THE CHRONIC

A NEW FORM of West Coast gangsta rap called "G-funk" came onto the hip-hop scene in 1992. This style had long, whiny-sounding notes produced by an electronic instrument called a synthesizer and a slower, laid-back sound that felt more like the beaches of California than the concrete streets of the city. This new style of

▲ Dr. Dre

gangsta rap was produced by Dr. Dre, a founding member of N.W.A. His 1992 debut album, *The Chronic,* hit the radio airwaves and hip-hop fans all over the world were hooked. The first single from the album, "Nuthin' but a 'G' Thang," featuring a young rapper called Snoop Doggy Dogg, reached number 3 on the *Billboard* Hot 100 chart and number 1 on the R&B/Hip-Hop chart. The song was so popular that it became a kind of anthem for West Coast hip-hop culture.

Dr. Dre is one of the most powerful West Coast hip-hop rappers and producers of all time. *The Chronic* created a sound that would set the tone for many rappers to follow with its easygoing, almost dreamy electronic beats that earned California and West Coast rappers their rightful place in hip-hop culture.

SNOOP DOGGY DOGG'S DEBUT ALBUM, *DOGGYSTYLE*

ANOTHER RAPPER WHO had a unique rapping flow was the young Long Beach, California, rapper Snoop Doggy Dogg (whose name is now Snoop Dogg). After Snoop Dogg appeared on Dr. Dre's *The Chronic* in 1992, he released his first album, *Doggystyle,* a year later.

Dr. Dre took young Snoop Dogg under his wing and produced the beats with him, giving *Doggystyle* a similar sound and style of the music of *The Chronic.* The thing that made Snoop Dogg different was his slightly slowed down singsongy rap flow that was still very confident, but not as aggressive as rappers who came before him.

Important West Coast Rappers

Too $hort

Warren G

Nate Dogg

E-40

Ras Kass

Cypress Hill

MC Hammer

Del the Funky Homosapien

The Pharcyde

The Coup

Jay Rock

Madlib

Kendrick Lamar

Spice 1

The D.O.C.

▲ Cypress Hill

The easygoing sound and California **vibe** of *Doggystyle* drew even more dedicated fans to West Coast hip-hop as the album hit number 1 on the *Billboard* 200 chart. Album sales were through the roof, and like Dr. Dre, Snoop Dogg not only became a star but a hip-hop icon. Today, Snoop Dogg has sold nearly sixty million albums around the world since the beginning of his career. He is a household name and people across all backgrounds, cultures, and communities love him for his humor and friendly personality despite his aggressive lyrics.

As he grew older, younger rappers began calling him "Uncle Snoop" because he was a person who cared for them and supported them in their careers. He is a treasure to hip-hop culture and played an important role in making hip-hop the worldwide music genre it is today.

East Coast versus West Coast

(1995-1997)

There was a sad time in hip-hop history when rappers from the East Coast and West Coast of the United States became very angry with one another and as a result lives were lost.

In the late 1980s gangsta rap was just beginning to develop on each coast around the same time. But as West Coast hip-hop began to grow and attract attention from millions of people all over the world in the early 1990s, the rappers of the West Coast felt that the East Coast hip-hop community did not respect them for their accomplishments. They felt they were not treated as equals and that the East Coast thought they were a lesser community of rappers and artists.

East Coast rappers, particularly those from New York, understood that their city was the birthplace of hip-hop and rap music and they wanted it to always be made clear they were the innovators.

TUPAC AND BIGGIE SMALLS

AS TIME WENT on, the world began to look at the crumbling relationship between two rappers, one from the East Coast and one from the West.

The Notorious B.I.G., also known as Biggie Smalls, was from Brooklyn, New York. He was

supported by his producer and founder of his record label, Bad Boy Records, Sean "Puffy" Combs. Sean Combs was also his good friend and together, as the world looked on, they became representatives of the East Coast hip-hop community.

In the early 1990s, Biggie and Tupac Shakur got into a disagreement. It added to the feeling that the East Coast and West Coast were against each other. The tension lasted for years.

Sadly, Tupac died in 1996 and then Biggie died in 1997. The world was very sad to see these rappers lose their lives. Murals and images of both artists are painted all over the world and their musical influence and legacy is like no one else's in hip-hop.

▲ The Notorious B.I.G. and Tupac Shakur

EAST COAST AND WEST COAST COME TOGETHER IN PEACE

IN 1996, LOUIS FARRAKHAN, the leader of the Nation of Islam, brought together leaders from the East and West Coast hip-hop communities to talk about peace soon after Tupac died. The leaders came together again after Biggie Smalls passed away.

Shortly after Biggie's and Tupac's deaths, rappers from the East Coast and West Coast, particularly Snoop Dogg, Sean "Diddy" Combs, and others, came together to create a truce that is honored to this day. Rappers from the East Coast and West Coast are still proud of where they come from, but they have promised to never hurt another person because of where they come from.

▲ **West Coast top to bottom: Warren G, Snoop Dogg, Tupac Shakur, Eazy-E, Ice Cube**

MISSING YOU

ON MARCH 27, 1997, Sean Combs; Biggie's wife, Faith Evans; and the Bad Boy Records R&B group came together to release "Missing You" in memory of Biggie. The song was also included on Sean Combs's album *No Way Out,* and it sampled the 1993 hit song "Every Breath You Take" by British rock group The Police.

The song went to number one in 16 countries including the United States, spending several weeks on the top Billboard 100 Charts. The song's international success was a true testament to how many people truly felt the loss of Biggie Smalls. The song's touching lyrics gave fans around the world—both children and adults—the healing they needed.

▲ **East Coast top to bottom: LL Cool J, Biggie Smalls, KRS-ONE, Mobb Deep (Prodigy and Havoc)**

The Growth of Southern Hip-Hop

Even though hip-hop began in the Bronx, it soon began to spring up all over the United States. Hip-hop began to emerge in the South in the mid-1980s; today, hip-hop artists from the region have come to dominate the radio, causing the world to hear hip-hop in new ways.

THE GETO BOYS

THE GETO BOYS, a trio from Houston, Texas, were one of the first southern hip-hop groups to achieve success similar to those from New York City. Their first album was called *Making Trouble* and was released on Rap-A-Lot Records, a Houston-based label started by James Prince, also known as J. Prince.

Making Trouble didn't make a big splash or sell a lot of records, so to help the group grow and attract more fans and listeners J. Prince decided to bring together a new lineup of rappers for the group. He connected Houston rappers Scarface and Willie D and dancer and rapper Bushwick Bill to replace earlier members DJ Ready Red and Prince Johnny C.

The Geto Boys worked hard and released *Grip It! On That Other Level* in 1989. The album had a lot of very violent lyrics and was disrespectful to women. Because of their very heavy and intense lyrics, the album was the beginning of what would become called "horrorcore," which was a style of rap that was dark and a bit scary.

Fans connected with the second album much more and the Geto Boys caught the attention of Rick Rubin of Def Jam Recordings who helped the Geto Boys release a remix album called *The Geto Boys*. The group received their first hit song with "Mind Playing Tricks on Me" from their 1991 album, *We Can't Be Stopped,* hitting number 23 on the *Billboard* Hot 100 chart.

Once the Geto Boys found their footing with Def Jam, they went on to have a successful career and released several entertaining and strange music videos for the eerie music they were playing. The Geto Boys are noted to be one of the first southern hip-hop groups to connect with a wide audience.

▲ **The Geto Boys**

MIAMI BASS

LUTHER "LUKE SKYYWALKER" Campbell is a record producer and rapper who made the Miami bass style of hip-hop a popular subgenre. Miami bass began in the mid-1980s and early 1990s with the group 2 Live Crew. This style of music opened doors for Miami-based rappers, like Trick Daddy, Trina, and Rick Ross, to become huge successes.

Lil Jon is a well-known Miami-based rapper and producer whose spin on the Miami bass sound took the world by storm in the 2000s.

HOUSTON HIP-HOP

THE SUCCESS OF J. Prince's work with Rap-A-Lot Records laid some groundwork for other Houston- and Texas-based hip-hop artists to come onto the scene. UGK was a hip-hop duo whose members were rapper and producer Pimp C and rapper Bun B. UGK had a very southern sound and used elements of country music, creating a new form of hip-hop called "country rap." Because of their unique style, they received a record deal with Jive Records and released their debut album *Too Hard to Swallow* in 1992.

▶ J. Prince

DJ SCREW

▲ DJ Screw

DJ SCREW WAS a music producer who had a special talent. He would take songs and slow them down to an extremely slow tempo and mix up the lyrics to songs. His style was interesting and had never been heard before. This style of remixes and music production was called "chopped and screwed." Even though DJ Screw died in 2000, his sound can be heard in later Houston hip-hop artists like Paul Wall, Chamillionaire, and Slim Thug.

NEW ORLEANS

IN 1992, A form of hip-hop music called "bounce" emerged from New Orleans due to the local success of a song called "Where Dey at?" by DJ Irv and MC T. Tucker. Bounce had a fun sound that included bassy drum patterns and handclaps that sounded like second line parades. A second line parade is a community feel where dancers and musicians follow the main line of a parade, which is led by an array of horns.

CASH MONEY RECORDS

IN 1991, TWO brothers, Ronald "Slim" Williams and Bryan "Birdman" Williams, started a record label called Cash Money Records. Along with other young New Orleans–based record labels, Parkway Pumpin' and Pack Records, a number of artists like Juvenile, Cheeky Blakk, Lil Slim, Pimp Daddy, Magnolia Slim, Everlasting Hitman, Silky Slim, and others were able to release their music and find new listeners.

MYSTIKAL AND CASH MONEY RECORDS

MYSTIKAL IS A rapper from New Orleans. He had success with his debut album, *Mystikal,* on a local record label called Big Boy in 1994. In 1995, he signed to Jive, and later Master P's No Limit Records and released his second album, *Unpredictable,* which sold many albums, landing on number 3 on the *Billboard* 200 chart and number 1 on the R&B/Hip-Hop chart. He was very popular and released a lot of music under the No Limit Records label, which had become a community of other New Orleans hip-hop artists like Soulja Slim, Silkk the Shocker, Mercedes, Mia X, C-Murder, and others.

MASTER P

MASTER P IS a rapper, producer, and entrepreneur who started the label No Limit Records. In the late 1990s and early 2000s, this record company dominated the radio and music television. As a rapper, he released his debut album, *Get Away Clean,* in 1991 and continued to release his own music for years. Master P is known to be one of the best businesspeople in the music industry. No Limit Records became very successful and made him a leader in the New Orleans hip-hop scene. Albums by No Limit Records had a similar look to them so you could recognize them without having to think about it. This helped No Limit stick in the minds of music listeners and buyers all over the country.

▲ Master P

MEMPHIS AND THREE 6 MAFIA

THREE 6 MAFIA is a hip-hop group from Memphis, Tennessee, that came together in 1991. The members of the group—DJ Paul and Juicy J and featuring male rappers Lord Infamous, Gangsta Boo, and Project Pat—became known for their horrorcore hip-hop style similar to the Geto Boys but with heavy, slow beats, and an intense layering of sounds. The debut album, *Mystic Stylez,* is known among rappers and fans to be an important album in southern hip-hop history. Three 6 Mafia sold millions of albums through the early aughts.

The group won an Academy Award for Best Original Song in 2006 for "It's Hard Out Here for a Pimp," which was the theme song for the VH1 hip-hop film *Hustle & Flow*.

ATLANTA

IN 1989, ANTONIO "L.A." REID and Kenneth "Babyface" Edmonds moved to Atlanta to start LaFace Records. Their arrival brought incredible opportunities for musicians to get signed to a record label. Artists like TLC, Goodie Mob, Cool Breeze, and Outkast put the Atlanta music scene on the map and went on to have long and influential careers. The hip-hop group Arrested Development was truly the first to break out to national listeners in 1992.

▲ Outkast (André 3000, born André Lauren Benjamin, and Antwan "Big Boi" Patton)

▲ Three 6 Mafia

SO SO DEF RECORDINGS

IN 1992, MUSIC producer Jermaine Dupri founded the record label, So So Def Recordings. The record label is known for its successful teen hip-hop duo Kris Kross and rapper Da Brat. His production style was well-known in the hip-hop world, and he spawned many hit songs.

▲ Kris Kross

VIRGINIA BEACH

HIGHLY INFLUENTIAL RAPPERS and producers Tim "Timbaland" Mosley and Missy Elliott both came from Virginia, and they brought an innovative sound to hip-hop. Their playful and complicated beats and rhymes were outside the box, making them very appealing to hip-hop fans all over the world. The Neptunes, who included Pharrell Williams and Chad Hugo, produced important hip-hop songs of the early aughts. Pharrell went on to become a successful solo artist, recording the groundbreaking track "Happy" in 2013.

Hip-hop music from the southern region of the United States of America blew over the mainstream and hip-hop worlds like a cool breeze, leading with many hits and different sounds and styles in the late 1990s through the start of the next century.

OUTKAST

THE ATLANTA-BASED hip-hop duo Outkast is one of the most popular hip-hop groups in history. Forming in 1992, they are most known to their seminal albums *Aquemini* (1998) and *Stankonia* (2000), which were both commercial successes. Their 1996 album, *ATLiens,* should also be noted as an important album and an experimental spin on the early foundation of **trap music**.

Their otherworldly sounds, laid-back style, and powerful mix of rock, jazz, and other genres later in their careers made them one of the most successful acts to this day.

The Evolution of Modern Hip-Hop

(1994–2003)

Hip-hop in the mid-1990s was thriving. West Coast hip-hop dominated in the early 1990s but toward the mid-1990s, East Coast rappers began to attract attention back into their direction with the entrance of legendary rappers and groups like Nas, Wu-Tang Clan, Mobb Deep, and Jay Z.

Chicago-based rappers like Common and Kanye West also began their long and historical careers during this time period as well.

▲ **Common**

NASIR "NAS" JONES

IN 1994, A young rapper named Nasir Jones, better known as Nas, created one of the most important hip-hop albums of all time—*Illmatic*—with the help of iconic producers from hip-hop's golden age. Other rappers of this scene and era include Q-Tip of A Tribe Called Quest, Pete Rock, Large Professor, L.E.S., and DJ Premier.

Nas had attracted attention following his 1991 debut live performance where he rapped mind-blowing rhymes among some of New York's leading rappers. After signing with Columbia Records, he set out to create a masterpiece that was worthy of his incredible talent for storytelling and poetry. A lot of people believed in him and his producers gave him the best support a young rapper could ever ask for.

The album *Illmatic* was like a storybook. Nas rhymed about the world he saw through his own eyes. Growing up in the Queensbridge housing project in Queens, New York City, Nas experienced

scenes of violence, drugs, gang activity, and crime. His lyrics were very wise and, even though he was just a teenager, his words were that of an old man who had lived many years. He was compared to rapper Rakim, but he had a more visual and artistic spin to the rhymes he wrote.

Illmatic is one of the most important classic hip-hop albums in music history, making Nas one of the best rappers to ever enter the genre. Nas continues to rap and is considered to be one of the best rappers anyone has or will ever see.

▲ Nasir "Nas" Jones

WU-TANG CLAN

THE WU-TANG CLAN is a group like no other. Members include Raekwon, RZA, GZA, Method Man, Ol' Dirty Bastard, Ghostface Killah, Inspectah Deck, Masta Killa, and U-God. They burst onto the scene with their 1993 debut album, *Enter the Wu-Tang (36 Chambers)*.

Heavily influenced by martial arts and kung fu films, the Wu-Tang Clan's large number of rappers didn't stop them from making amazing music that people could understand and enjoy with surprise and excitement. All the rappers had their own style and came together to bring about a new movement in hip-hop.

Hip-hop fans felt they were a part of a family when they listened to the Wu-Tang Clan. Kids all over the United States and the world listened to the gritty rhymes about the streets of New York.

Each member also released solo albums and achieved success in their own right with Method Man, Raekwon, Ghostface Killah, RZA, and GZA all moving forward to have long careers in rapping and in creating music for films.

The Wu-Tang Clan brought community and a martial arts–spin to their hip-hop world and they are loved for it. They will never be forgotten in the time line of hip-hop history.

▲ Wu-Tang Clan

MOBB DEEP

LIKE NAS, RAPPER Havoc (Kejuan Waliek Muchita) of the hip-hop group Mobb Deep grew up in the Queensbridge housing project. The other half of the duo, Prodigy (Albert Johnson), was a talented lyricist who had a mysterious and serious rap style that made him very interesting to listen to and understand.

They had a heavy and dark sound that echoed their surroundings. Their hard-core lyrics revealed stories of violence and betrayal. Mobb Deep is an important hip-hop group of the mid-1990s that helped bring listeners back to listening to New York hip-hop after the world had directed their ears to mostly the West Coast hip-hop variety only a couple of years before.

J DILLA, SLUM VILLAGE, AND THE SOULQUARIANS

THE DETROIT-BASED PRODUCER J Dilla was one of the most important producers in hip-hop history. In the mid-1990s he produced albums for musicians and groups like De La Soul, Busta Rhymes, and the Pharcyde.

J. Dilla was a member of the group Slum Village, which released their debut album entitled *Fan-Tas-Tic (Vol. 1)* in 2000. He also joined the hip-hop/soul collective the Soulquarians and this was when the producer's music really became recognized by listeners from all over the world.

The Soulquarians consisted of Erykah Badu, J Dilla, Q-Tip of A Tribe Called Quest, James Poyser, Talib Kweli, Mos Def, Common, Bilal, Pino Palladino, D'Angelo, Roy Hargrove, and Questlove of the Roots. J Dilla worked with these artists in the revamped hip-hop landscape and built an offshoot style of music called "neo soul."

J Dilla died in 2006, but as time went on, hip-hop lovers became more and more interested in the hip-hop production work he had done. There are many albums of his that were released after he died. His name and contributions to hip-hop will live on well into the future.

▲ Mobb Deep

JAY Z

THE BROOKLYN-BORN RAPPER Shawn Carter, better known as Jay Z, began his career by starting Roc-A-Fella Records in 1995. He had been through a lot in his early life. He had sold drugs and, due to his activity, had been shot on the streets of New York City. But because of this he was street-smart and savvy, so he decided to release his 1996 debut album, *Reasonable Doubt,* on his own label, Roc-A-Fella. He had great connections with Biggie Smalls, Mary J. Blige, and others who came together to make music for him on his first album.

Reasonable Doubt did well and was number 23 on the *Billboard* 200 chart, but this was just the beginning. Jay Z went on to become one of the most powerful and admired rappers in hip-hop history.

He made some of the most important hip-hop albums, including 2001's *The Blueprint,* which included four songs produced by the talented up-and-coming rapper and incredible beat-maker, Kanye West.

Jay Z's intelligent and confident rhymes, strong stature, and vision of where hip-hop could go made him a leader in the hip-hop world. In 2004, he became the president of Def Jam Recordings making sure the label continued its long history of putting out some of the world's most important and influential hip-hop music in the world.

He is now said to be a "GOAT," or the greatest (rapper) of all time. He is one of the wealthiest Black people in the world. He married the famous singer Beyoncé in 2008 making them one of the most powerful couples in Black music.

▲ Shawn Carter, aka Jay Z

EMINEM

THE LATE 1990S also welcomed the music of another hip-hop icon, Eminem. He was born Marshall Bruce Mathers III in St. Joseph, Missouri, and got involved in hip-hop when he was in high school in the Detroit area. He would sneak into his friend Proof's neighboring high school just to hear him rap battle with other kids in the lunchroom. He was very inspired by hip-hop culture at the beginning of his career, and he called himself MC Double M. Throughout the late 1980s and early 1990s, he rapped with a couple of groups and worked hard to record his first self-titled EP. EP is short for "extended play album," and it features one to five songs. The EP grabbed the attention of a record company called F.B.T. Productions who helped him release his first album, *Infinite,* in 1995.

Eminem's lyrical style and voice didn't truly connect with fans until the release of his second EP, the *Slim Shady EP,* where he became a character called Slim Shady. This gave him the ability to rap about the things that he would not have rapped about under his own name. Slim Shady gave him bravery to push his lyrics, which were sometimes violent and scary. Nonetheless, Eminem worked even harder and traveled to Los Angeles to compete in the famous hip-hop competition the Rap Olympics. He did a great job and got second place, and caught the attention of a person at Interscope Records who gave Eminem's *Slim Shady EP* to Dr. Dre.

Dr. Dre was so impressed with Eminem's creativity and out-of-this-world gift for rapping that he signed him to his label, Aftermath Entertainment.

With Dr. Dre's help, Eminem released *The Slim Shady LP* in 1999. The album was loved by many all over the world, making it one of the most successful albums of the year. Hip-hop culture connected to Eminem's mix of silliness and humor and dark and almost horror film–like lyrics. The success of his first album was just the beginning. His 2001 second studio album, *The Marshall Mathers LP,* sold over one million copies in its first week out. The album set records for the fastest-selling hip-hop and solo album of all time. From then on Eminem became a global icon.

He is also known for reaching hip-hop fans in parts of the United States like the Midwest that weren't as familiar with hip-hop. Eminem has sold an amazing amount of albums and worked closely with Dr. Dre and his labelmate 50 Cent on songs that took the United States and world by storm.

▲ Marshall Bruce Mathers III, aka Eminem

50 CENT

MUCH LIKE DR. DRE discovered and launched the career of Eminem, Eminem did the same for South Jamaica, Queens, New York, rapper Curtis James Jackson III, better known as 50 Cent. 50 Cent had a long and tough road to becoming one of the most powerful artists in hip-hop history.

In the late 1990s, Jam Master Jay of Run-DMC treated 50 Cent like a little brother and taught him how to write strong hip-hop songs. 50 Cent got his first chance to rap on a recording in 1998 on a song called "React" by the hip-hop trio Onyx.

He was on his way when he signed a record deal with Columbia Records but his music was never released. He wrote a song with lyrics that offended many people and had a hard time getting other record labels to sign him and put out his music. But 50 Cent had a plan. He independently released more than thirty mixtapes and let the world hear his music on his own terms.

But it was his 2002 **mixtape**, *Guess Who's Back?,* that made fans really excited and caught the ears of someone at Eminem's record label, Shady Records. He soon met with Eminem and Dr. Dre and signed a million-dollar record deal with the hip-hop icons. His debut album, *Get Rich or Die Tryin',* was released in 2003 and debuted at number 1 on the *Billboard* 200 chart. His single "In da Club" was a fun dance hit that drew in hip-hop lovers.

50 Cent has gone on to become a leader in hip-hop entertainment, releasing successful albums and producing television and film. Today, he is one of the most well-known and admired rappers in hip-hop history.

▲ Curtis James Jackson III, aka 50 Cent

LIL WAYNE

DWAYNE MICHAEL CARTER JR., better known as Lil Wayne, was a rambunctious young man who found himself in the middle of the New Orleans hip-hop scene. His talent and light shone so bright that at only eight years old, he was discovered by record producer Bryan "Baby" Williams, better known to the world as Birdman.

Birdman treated Lil Wayne like a younger brother and became his mentor. He taught Wayne the ins and outs of the hip-hop world and by age twelve, Lil Wayne had a record deal with Cash Money Records in 1994.

He became a member of the Hot Boys whose other members included B.G., Turk, and Juvenile, and in 1997 they released their debut album, *Get It How U Live!*. The group was very popular in the southern region of the United States where they were able to garner a strong fan base. But it was their second studio album, 1999's *Guerrilla Warfare*, that was their biggest success climbing to number 5 on the *Billboard* 200 chart and number 1 on the R&B/Hip-Hop Albums chart.

Lil Wayne gained popularity and when he released his solo debut album, *Tha Block Is Hot,* in 1999 the album quickly went platinum, meaning it sold over one million copies. Over the next five years, Lil Wayne released three more studio albums and founded the Young Money Entertainment record label as an imprint of Cash Money Records.

In 2008 he released *Tha Carter III,* which sold more than one million copies in the first week. Along with being featured on many hit songs with

artists like Rick Ross, T-Pain, T.I., Akon, and others, he was also at the top of the charts with a number of popular R&B and hip-hop songs.

In 2009, Lil Wayne signed a young rising rapper named Drake to his record label. He helped Drake become one of the most listened to rappers of all time. He also signed Nicki Minaj who went on to have an amazing music career. The three artists have rapped on songs together throughout the ten-plus years they have been working together.

The dawn of the twenty-first century ushered in a more diverse and polished hip-hop, including Lil Wayne, who continues to make music into the 2020s. It brought hip-hop to the forefront of mainstream music, making it the most popular genre of music across the planet.

▲ Dwayne Michael Carter Jr., aka Lil Wayne

Hip-Hop Becomes Popular Music

(2003-2022)

Many of the artists who got their start in the late 1990s became major successes in the first decade of the new century. Eminem, Jay Z, and 50 Cent all went on to run record labels of their own to support new talent. They were big influences on popular artists of the 2010s and 2020s, like Drake, Kanye West, Kendrick Lamar, Young Thug, and Travis Scott.

KANYE WEST

In the early aughts, the talented young producer Kanye West was brought on by Jay Z's record label, Roc-A-Fella Records, to be a regular producer. His beats were different and stood out. He had an amazing ear for music and produced songs on some of Jay Z's most important records like 2001's *The Blueprint* and also produced popular R&B songs for Alicia Keys and Janet Jackson.

The beginning of his career was going well but in 2002, Kanye was injured in a serious car accident and had to have his jaw wired shut. This didn't make him give up. Kanye decided to rap while his mouth was wired shut, sharing what happened in the accident. The song was called "Through the Wire," which was well received by fans and became the foundation for his debut studio album, *The College Dropout*, released in 2004.

Although record labels were unsure whether he would be a successful rapper, Kanye's creative rhymes and supreme production skills made him

▲ J. Cole

a wonderful performer to listen to and watch. *The College Dropout* album hit number 2 on the *Billboard* 200 chart and was nominated for ten Grammy Awards. His early collection of albums, including 2005's *Late Registration*, 2007's *Graduation,* and 2008's *808s & Heartbreak* are considered masterpieces that influenced a new generation of rappers. He used a mix of orchestral music and electronic sounds to make his songs very different from what was being played on the radio at the time. Because of all this, Kanye became a leader and innovator in hip-hop in the first decades of the twenty-first century.

He released his eleventh studio album, *Donda,* in 2022 and even though he has struggled for many years with mental health, he is one of the most groundbreaking rappers and producers of all time.

▲ Kanye West

DRAKE

A YOUNG ACTOR named Aubrey Drake Graham, better known as Drake, began his career in the entertainment industry on the popular teen drama *Degrassi: The Next Generation* from 2001 to 2008. But Drake had bigger plans for himself. Deep down he wanted to become a rapper.

He worked hard on his rhymes and in 2006, he self-released a mixtape called *Room for Improvement*. The album didn't have very much success. His own label and fashion label called October's Very Own released another mixtape called *Comeback Season* in 2007, but it wasn't until the release of 2009's *So Far Gone* that Drake truly began to break through and grab the attention of fans and the music industry. The first two singles from the album were called "Best I Ever Had" and "Successful." They became incredibly popular and it is said that record labels were fighting one another to sign him.

Drake decided to sign with Lil Wayne's Young Money Entertainment and released his first studio album, *Thank Me Later,* in 2010. Then, the iconic, unique, and deeply important album *Take Care* was released in 2011.

Take Care wasn't Drake's most successful album, but it was beautifully produced. It sounded unlike anything anyone had ever heard, with elements of global music in it. He had made what some would call his greatest album, although the 2013 follow-up, *Nothing Was the Same,* was a success and every album that followed broke record after record for the most streams, which is when a song is played through apps like Spotify

and Apple Music. Drake was the first artist to hit one billion streams with his iconic popular hit song "God's Plan" from his 2018 studio album, *Scorpion.*

Drake's 2022 album, *Certified Lover Boy,* broke the record for most streams in a twenty-four-hour period, with 153 million streams. His 2018 album, *Scorpion,* had held the record with 132 million streams. He is also the first artist to achieve fifty billion streams on the music platform Spotify in 2021.

Drake is by far one of the most listened to rappers in modern hip-hop. Because of online streaming platforms, he has been able to reach more people than others before him. The world loves listening to Drake and he continues to give his fans great music.

▲ Aubrey Drake Graham, aka Drake

Drake's Accomplishments Throughout His Career

2015: Mixtapes *If You're Reading This It's Too Late* and *What a Time to Be Alive* both reach number 1 on the *Billboard* 200, making him the first hip-hop artist to have two projects do that in the same year since 2004.

2016: Fourth studio album, *Views,* spends thirteen nonconsecutive weeks at number 1, making him the first male solo artist to do so in a decade.

2017: Mixtape *More Life* becomes highest-ever streamed album in twenty-four hours on both Apple Music and Spotify. And he wins thirteen awards at the Billboard Music Awards, the record for most wins in a single show.

2018: "God's Plan" breaks Apple Music and Spotify first-day streaming records. He becomes the rapper with the most top 10 hits on the *Billboard* Hot 100. "Nice for What" replacing "God's Plan" at number 1 makes him the first artist ever to have a new number 1 debut replace a former number 1 debut. *Scorpion* release breaks *More Life*'s records on Spotify and Apple Music, and it is the first to ever cross one billion streams in the first week. With seven simultaneous singles charting in the top 10, Drake breaks the Beatles' record of five from 1964.

2020: "Toosie Slide" debuts at number 1, making him the first male artist to have three songs debut at number 1 on the *Billboard* Hot 100.

2021: In January, he becomes the first artist to surpass fifty billion combined streams on Spotify.

2022: *Certified Lover Boy* breaks the record for most streams in a twenty-four-hour time period, with 153 million.

T-PAIN

FAHEEM RASHEED NAJM, better known as hip-hop star T-Pain, was born in Tallahassee, Florida. He is known for his unique use of an electronic feature called "**auto-tune**." Auto-tune changes the pitch of a singer's voice making it connect with a musical note and then stretching it to make it sound like it is slipping on a wet slide. His use of this sound effect changed hip-hop music forever. New artists coming up behind him like Future and Travis Scott used this new tool and established artists like Snoop Dogg and Kanye West began to experiment and release music after being inspired by T-Pain's new hip-hop style.

Other rappers and musicians weren't the only ones who were interested in T-Pain's use of auto-tune. Listeners and music fans wanted to be a part of the new trend as well. In 2009, iPhone created an app called I Am T-Pain, which allowed users to put auto-tune on their own voices directly from their phone.

In 2004, T-Pain was discovered by Akon, the influential musical artist from Senegal, a country in West Africa. Akon had found success in the American music market and heard a song by T-Pain that had been inspired by Akon's 2004 single "Locked Up." He signed T-Pain to his record label, Konvict Muzik, and in 2005, he released his first album, *Rappa Ternt Sanga*.

Through the late 2010s, T-Pain continued to release music for his fans. His unique music made him a leader in the world of hip-hop music production. He will forever be remembered as the artist who opened the door for a new sound to

emerge, moving hip-hop forward into the modern era and well into the future.

TYLER, THE CREATOR

TYLER GREGORY OKONMA, better known as Tyler, the Creator, got his start rapping and producing for the hip-hop music collective Odd Future in 2007. The collective was made up of a group of very different, experimental, and creative young lyricists who were also very talented in creating interesting music videos and comedy television series.

▲ Faheem Rasheed Najm, aka T-Pain

Following the release of their debut mixtape, *The Odd Future Tape,* in 2008, Tyler decided to branch out and release his own solo mixtape, *Bastard,* in 2009. Tyler's music was dark and heavy, and was connected to the horrorcore genre of hip-hop music. His music production was interesting and his videos were colorful, like the early work of Eminem.

With a couple of years of hard work, Tyler, the Creator and Odd Future were beginning to gain attention. With the support of influential rappers like Jay Z and Rick Ross, and powerful industry professionals, they received a record deal in 2011.

Tyler, the Creator's first solo album, *Goblin,* was released in 2011. The album wasn't that successful, but people could clearly see Tyler had interesting ideas. He launched the record label, Odd Future Records, and released the Odd Future album *Wolf* in 2013. As he moved through his career Tyler slowly became very influential on his own.

The horrorcore-style lyrics and bleak-sounding musical beats of his early albums began to become a bit easier to listen to. His rhymes became less angry and Tyler began to adopt an alternative style of dress and musical expression similar to the uniqueness of André 3000 of Outkast.

Tyler's hard work and ability to grow and refine his music began to bring him worldwide success in the late 2010s and 2020s. In 2019, his fifth album, *Igor,* hit number 1 on the *Billboard* 200 chart. The album also won the Grammy award for Best Rap Album. In 2021, he released his sixth album, *Call Me If You Get Lost,* which also hit number 1 on the *Billboard* charts. The album, which featured artists like Lil Wayne, Pharrell Williams, and Ty Dolla Sign,

won Tyler the Grammy for Best Rap Album for the second year in a row.

Tyler, the Creator began his career as an intelligent and innovative young man. Some say he had a lot of anger. His lyrics were so dark in his early work that government officials from England did not allow him to tour his music around the country for some time. But over the years, Tyler grew into a mature and smart recording artist and producer who has achieved worldwide success and inspired music fans worldwide.

▲ **Tyler Gregory Okonma, aka Tyler, the Creator**

TRAVIS SCOTT

JACQUES BERMON WEBSTER II, better known by his rap name Travis Scott, released his first mixtape, *Owl Pharaoh,* in 2013. His music had deep beats and instrumentals with a flowing, layered rapping and singing style. It grabbed the attention of Kanye West, who helped re-form *Owl Pharoah,* which featured the vocals of R&B hip-hop singer Wale and a remix from Pusha T. Pusha T is also an artist and is the current president of Kanye West's record label, G.O.O.D. Music.

In 2014, Travis Scott released his second mixtape, *Days Before Rodeo,* which featured artists like T.I., Young Thug, and Migos. He toured the music from the album with Young Thug across the country. The tour was successful and opened the door for him to follow his mixtapes with his debut studio album, *Rodeo.* The album landed at number 3 on the *Billboard* 200 chart and number 1 on the R&B/Hip-Hop chart, making him an important up-and-coming rapper in the 2010s. His second album, *Birds in the Trap Sing McKnight,* became his first number-one album. His third album, the award-winning *Astroworld,* was also number one.

Travis Scott's flowing, experimental hip-hop, where he mixed echoes, music, and vocals gave him a very recognizable sound. He had a style of his own that moved hip-hop deeper into a more otherworldly sound. His music helped define the sound of the 2010s, which was futuristic and interesting to listen to.

▲ Jacques Bermon Webster II, aka Travis Scott

TRAP MUSIC

TRAP MUSIC IS a subgenre (a more specific style) of hip-hop whose foundation is rooted in early southern hip-hop. The main instrument used to create the original sound was a drum machine called the Roland TR-808 drum machine. Also known as "808s," these electronic instruments were able to give a watery, swelling sound with heavy bass and accented low end notes.

YOUNG THUG

JEFFERY LAMAR WILLIAMS, also known as Young Thug, also helped define the southern trap hip-hop sound of the 2010s. Born in Atlanta, Georgia, he began his career in 2010, receiving the good fortune of being able to work with Kanye West, with whom he worked on a number of mixtapes. He released his first official studio album, *So Much Fun,* in 2019.

Along with Kanye West, Young Thug was very much supported by the southern hip-hop rapper Gucci Mane who signed Young Thug to his record label, 1017 Brick Squad or 1017 Records, in 2013. Over the years, Young Thug released a lot of music and played many live shows. His strong understanding of the Atlanta hip-hop sound allowed him to put his own touches on the music. Young Thug became a regular collaborator with Drake and other lead artists of the 2010s and his

mixtapes and singles like his song "Havana" with the popular Cuban pop artist Camila Cabello allowed him to hit the top of the *Billboard* charts years before his first album was released.

Young Thug grew through the ranks of the hip-hop world by crafting a style that connected to the southern hip-hop music that came before him and molding it into a crisp modern sound.

▲ Jeffery Lamar Williams, aka Young Thug

▲ Onika Tanya Maraj-Petty, aka Nicki Minaj

NICKI MINAJ

ONIKA TANYA MARAJ-PETTY, better known as Nicki Minaj to her many fans across the globe, became a lead hip-hop star in the 2010s. Her first mixtapes were *Playtime Is Over* from 2007, *Sucka Free* from 2008, and *Beam Me Up Scotty* from 2009. She scored a minor hit with the single "I Get Crazy" from her third mixtape, opening the opportunity for her to be discovered by Lil Wayne who signed her to his label, Young Money Entertainment, in 2009.

Nicki continued to be featured on singles but it was her guest verse on Kanye West's song "Monster," which also featured Rick Ross and Jay Z, where she truly broke through to audiences. Her verse on the male-dominated song was strong and forceful, and her lyrics were very impressive. She was able to stand as an equal in the midst of hip-hop powerhouses and laid a foundation to become a leader in her own right. Her 2010 debut studio album, *Pink Friday*, became the highest-selling first-week album for a woman's hip-hop album, making her a notable figure in hip-hop history.

Her second album, 2012's *Pink Friday: Roman Reloaded*, showed her ability to take on different personalities or "alter egos." Roman is one of Nicki's alter egos, which allowed her to rap about different topics and take on a different style to appeal to different rap fans.

Hip-Hop and Alter Egos

MUSICIANS ARE VERY creative. There are times when the art and music they make needs a more expansive outlet. When musicians become well-known, they sometimes feel limited in the creative work they do, so they create an alter ego, which is a character that reflects a part of themselves that many don't see.

Eminem, alter ego:
Slim Shady

2Pac, alter ego:
Makaveli

Nicki Minaj, alter ego:
Roman Zolanski

Sun Ra, alter ego:
Herman Blount

Donald Glover, alter ego:
Childish Gambino

▲ Donald Glover's alter ego, Childish Gambino

Nicki comes from a long line of woman rappers and hip-hop stars who broke through to change the male-dominated landscape of hip-hop history. Her style of dress and lyrical flow is mostly noted as being inspired by Lil' Kim. Lil' Kim was a musician who was popular in the 1990s. She had a deep raspy voice, heavy New York street lyrics, and ultra-feminine style. Foxy Brown was also a woman rapper who opened the doors for Nicki Minaj's style to shine through in the 2010s.

Nicki's third album, 2014's *The Pinkprint,* was nominated for three Grammy Awards and hit number 2 on the *Billboard* charts. Throughout her career, she has worked on songs with popular artists of the time like Ariana Grande, 2 Chainz, Madonna, and will.i.am.

Her album *Queen* was released in 2018 and highlights Nicki's gift as a recording artist. It is full of cool and complicated songs with different musical styles packed into each song. Her rhymes are fast-paced, smart, witty, and impressive.

Throughout the 2020s she has released a number of singles with artists like Doja Cat and A$AP Ferg, along with the reissue of her 2009 mixtape, *Beam Me Up Scotty,* in 2021. *Beam Me Up Scotty* became the highest charting debut for a woman-led mixtape and the highest charting reissued mixtape in hip-hop history.

KENDRICK LAMAR

KENDRICK LAMAR IS a rapper who changed the sound of hip-hop in the 2010s. He brought back the California style of the 1990s and combined it with "conscious hip-hop," where Lamar rapped about spirituality, his inner feelings, love, and the reality of his environment.

Kendrick was born Kendrick Lamar Duckworth in Compton, California. As a young boy, Kendrick was very inspired when he got to see Dr. Dre and Tupac Shakur film the music video for their huge hit song "California Love" in 1995. This experience led Kendrick to begin rapping under the hip-hop name K.Dot as a teenager. He worked very hard and by 2010 he released music and toured around the United States with influential artists like Tech N9ne and Jay Rock.

In 2010 he released the mixtape *Overly Dedicated*. He was then introduced to Dr. Dre who signed Kendrick to his record label, Aftermath Entertainment. In 2012, the world-changing, classic hip-hop album *Good Kid, M.A.A.D City* was released. It formally introduced Kendrick to a wider audience of hip-hop fans. His moving beats and wise lyrics made Kendrick an instant icon, bringing hip-hop to a new level. In 2013, he toured with Kanye West and lent lyrics to Eminem's album *The Marshall Mathers LP 2*.

In 2015 the album *To Pimp a Butterfly* would take the world by storm. It combined poetry, deeply touching beats, and the incredible imagination from Kendrick. Visionary producers like Thundercat, Flying Lotus, and Pharrell Williams worked on the album, which helped make it beautiful and different. The album won the Grammy Award for Best Rap Album and was nominated for six other awards.

His next album brought more excitement and was another well-produced, incredibly thoughtful album. It was a bit heavier and more minimal than the previous studio albums, but the world loved Kendrick and everything he was offering through his music.

In 2022, Kendrick rapped onstage at the Super Bowl LVI halftime show, performing in front millions of people.

Super Bowl LVI Halftime

THE SUPER BOWL LVI halftime show, which took place in February 2022, was a celebrated occasion for the hip-hop world at large.

The show featured Snoop Dogg, Dr. Dre, Eminem, Kendrick Lamar, 50 Cent, and deaf rappers Sean Forbes and Warren "WAWA" Snipe. It was one of the most televised performances in the world.

◀ Mary J. Blige, 50 Cent, Dr. Dre, and Snoop Dogg perform at the Super Bowl LVI Halftime Show.

J. COLE

JERMAINE LAMARR COLE, better known as J. Cole, was a good student who was inspired by artists like Nas and Tupac Shakur. He spent a lot of time writing and working on his craft as a rapper. His 2009 mixtape, *The Warm Up,* caught the attention of Jay Z, someone he had been trying to work with since the beginning of his career. He even had a chance to rap a verse on Jay Z's 2009 iconic "The Blueprint 3." He also rapped on songs with Talib Kweli, Mos Def, Jay Electronica, and Wale.

J. Cole was another leader, like Kendrick Lamar, in bringing "conscious rap" back to hip-hop. His rhymes are deeply thoughtful. J. Cole's hip-hop style also has elements of a number of hip-hop eras, mixing styles and beats, similar to the golden age of hip-hop and hip-hop's new school. This helped him become a leader of a new sound that was different from the trap-heavy, southern-rooted sound of the 2010s.

After releasing a number of mixtapes, J. Cole finally released his first studio album, *Cole World: The Sideline Story,* in 2011. His dedication paid off because it hit number 1 on the *Billboard* 200 chart. Earlier that year, Cole toured with Drake throughout the United Kingdom, making him even more popular.

Following the release of his second album, *Born Sinner,* in 2013 Cole wrote and released a political single called "Be Free" in 2014. It addressed the murder of Michael Brown, which took place in Ferguson, Missouri, earlier that year.

Cole traveled to protests about the murder to show support and engage with the community.

Cole released a number of albums throughout the 2010s. He returned to his political music by releasing the single "Snow on tha Bluff" in 2020 to speak his mind about the murder of another Black man named George Floyd.

He released his sixth studio album, *The Off-Season,* in 2021, which sold well, leading in the *Billboard* 200 chart.

J. Cole became iconic for his talent and understanding of the injustices for Black people in the United States of America. His poetry and thoughtfulness along with a strong awareness of himself made J. Cole a stand out as an important rapper in hip-hop history in the 2010s and 2020s.

FRANK OCEAN

CHRISTOPHER BREAUX, BETTER known as Frank Ocean, only released two studio albums in his career after working as a successful songwriter in the hip-hop/R&B music industry. He debut, *Channel Orange,* was released in 2012 on Def Jam Recordings and his independently released album, *Blonde,* followed in 2016. Both albums touched listeners with their otherworldly, unique sound.

As a member of the hip-hop collective Odd Future, Ocean had an experimental and minimal sound that other artists like Earl Sweatshirt and Syd the Kid in the collective shared in their music. *Blonde* was a Grammy Award–winning, widely respected album that truly launched his career.

The interesting thing about Frank Ocean is that he was very different in the ways he released music. He had a very hard time being a part of the world of the major record industry and quickly spread his wings by sharing his artistic abilities in ways other hip-hop music artists were not. He created the magazine called *Boys Don't Cry* in 2016.

In 2017, Ocean started the radio show Blonded Radio on Apple Music. He shared new music on it by Young Thug, Jay Z, and Tyler, the Creator and released some of his own singles, such as "Chanel" and "Provider." He also loves photography and did some photojournalism for an entertainment and tech online publication called *i-D*. In 2021, he created high-end jewelry under the brand Homer and released an almost ten-minute song on Blonded Radio.

▲ Christopher Breaux, aka Frank Ocean

Frank Ocean showed the world you don't have to be a super tough rapper who can only release music on big record labels. He has his own style and lives his life in a brave and interesting way. He is a very important artist of the 2010s and 2020s.

CARDI B

BELCALIS MARLENIS ALMÁNZAR, better known as Cardi B, is the only woman rapper to have number 1 songs and albums in the 2010s and 2020s in the history of hip-hop. She has dominated the charts and has become one of the most powerful women in hip-hop in modern times.

In 2017, she shared the stage with MC Lyte, Queen Latifah, the Lady of Rage, Lil' Kim, Monie Love, and Young M.A at Hot 97's Summer Jam, which was a powerfully groundbreaking moment for women in hip-hop.

Her 2018 debut album, the Grammy Award–winning *Invasion of Privacy*, changed the game in the 2010s. She worked with notable artists like Post Malone, Swae Lee, and Ed Sheeran and was one of the most sought after women to rap features on a number of songs by stars of the time. She was the first female solo artist to win Best Rap Album in 2019 for *Invasion of Privacy*. She also was nominated for twenty-one Billboard Music Awards that same year, the most nominations for any woman in the awards' history.

Cardi has described herself as a feminist, which is someone who believes women are equal to men and should be respected in every aspect of life: career, family, and cultural and social circles.

▲ Belcalis Marlenis Almánzar, aka Cardi B

Hip-Hop Today

Hip-hop has come a long way since it began in the South Bronx of New York City in the 1970s. It has changed and given the world an understanding of the Black artistic power of poetry, music, technology, and art. Hip-hop artists have found a way to communicate with people who are not from their communities, telling stories and looking inward to tell others what is going on in their hearts, minds, and bodies.

The growth and changes throughout hip-hop history have happened naturally, as rappers learned more about how to move the music forward with pure creativity and grace. The culture has gone through a lot of challenges as the conversation has revolved around how rappers write lyrics, specifically when it comes to lyrics that promote violence and are disrespectful of women. These conversations are important to have because everyone in the music industry should make sure that they are working hard to share the stage with diverse people of all identities. Artists of all genders have an important role to play in writing the next chapter of hip-hop history.

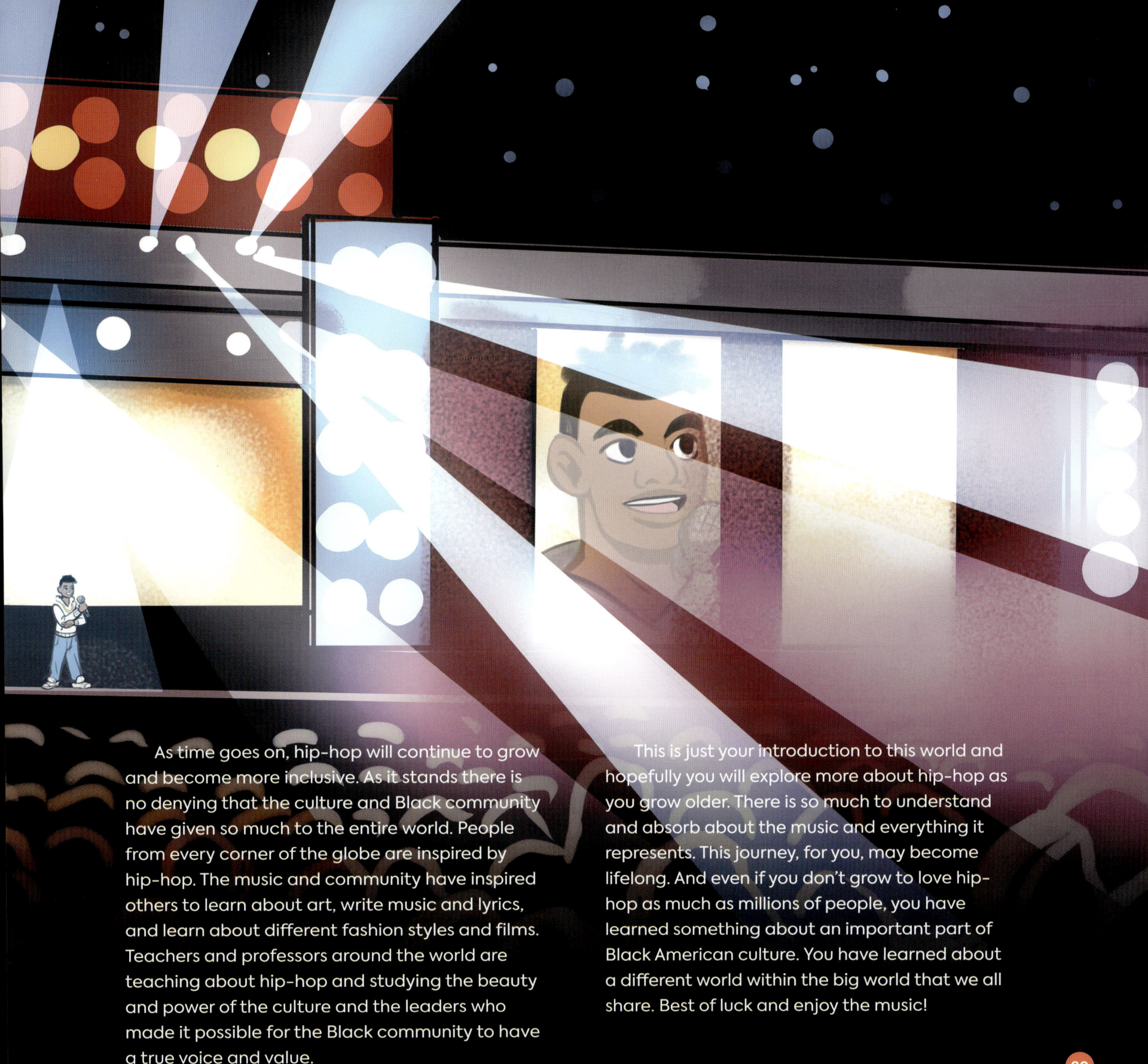

As time goes on, hip-hop will continue to grow and become more inclusive. As it stands there is no denying that the culture and Black community have given so much to the entire world. People from every corner of the globe are inspired by hip-hop. The music and community have inspired others to learn about art, write music and lyrics, and learn about different fashion styles and films. Teachers and professors around the world are teaching about hip-hop and studying the beauty and power of the culture and the leaders who made it possible for the Black community to have a true voice and value.

This is just your introduction to this world and hopefully you will explore more about hip-hop as you grow older. There is so much to understand and absorb about the music and everything it represents. This journey, for you, may become lifelong. And even if you don't grow to love hip-hop as much as millions of people, you have learned something about an important part of Black American culture. You have learned about a different world within the big world that we all share. Best of luck and enjoy the music!

Hip-Hop Glossary

HERE ARE SOME words you read about in the book. These words will help you understand how hip-hop music is made.

album—a collection of songs by a musician. Albums are usually sold and released by record companies.

answer record—a song that specifically refers to and "answers" the lyrics of another song.

auto-tune—computer software used to change the tune of vocals. Hip-hop started using auto-tune more at the beginning of the twenty-first century, allowing rappers and producers to alter their voices.

B side—when a musician releases a single from an album, it typically has two songs: an A side, a more popular song that gets more radio play and promotion, and a B side, a lesser known song on the same album.

beat—a beat is a sound that keeps the rhythm of a song intact. It is usually connected with a drum or other percussion sound.

beatbox—a simple or complex collection of beats a person creates with their mouth.

breakbeat—a sample of a drumbeat that is repeated, creating a syncopated rhythm.

break-dancer—a style of dance, mainly adopted by hip-hop culture that is inspired by gymnastics and martial arts. Dancers typically flip, split, and spin on their heads.

DJ—short for "disc jockey," who generally hosted radio shows, introducing and choosing specific songs for listeners. The MC (master of ceremonies, or emcee) had similar duties but hosted in-person events to hype a hip-hop event.

flow—the unique style of a rapper's vocals. Rappers can mix different vocal styles and rhythms to create different flows.

freestyle—improvised hip-hop lyrics.

hip-hop—a form of rap music, which was an early term for hip-hop.

hook—a catchy, singable phrase in a song. The hook is repeated throughout a hip-hop song, between verses. It is usually a danceable piece of music or a rhythmically pleasing sound.

lab—a term for a recording studio.

MC—a hip-hop lyricist; *see* DJ.

mixtape—made popular in hip-hop, a mixtape is typically an independently released collection of music. This means the artist released the music themselves without the help of a record company.

producer—the organizational leader in the recording studio. They can be creators of beats and hip-hop instrumentals and can also help lyricists write their lyrics.

rap—a term for the general genre of rap or hip-hop music, terms that can be used interchangeably. Rap music predates the postmodern hip-hop genre and can be found in African American music and music from the African diaspora. It includes spoken lyrics over electronic beats.

rapper—a performer of rap music. A lyricist who rhythmically speaks typically rhyming sentences over a beat-driven piece of music.

record label—a record label, or record company, is a company that sells musical recordings.

remix—a song that has been changed by a producer by taking an original song and adding their own style of musical production to it.

rhyme—lyrics that have similar syllables at the end of each line.

sample—a snippet of a song of any genre, used to create new hip-hop beats and music. It may be created by a sampler, an electronic instrument that is used to extract small sections of songs.

scratch—a DJ moving a vinyl record back and forth under the needle of a turntable.

single—a piece of music for promotional material of a full album that includes an A side (a lead single) and a B side (a song that record labels like but don't primarily push to be heard to represent a new album). When vinyl was invented, singles would be pressed on 45s or 7-inch vinyls that held only a couple minutes of music on each side. Each side of the vinyl would have one song.

trap music—a subgenre of hip-hop rooted in the southern music scene of the late 1990s.

vibe—a style of hip-hop that creates an emotional experience within the listener.

Further Reading

Hip Hop Speaks to Children: 50 Inspiring Poems with a Beat by Nikki Giovanni, Alicia Vergel de Dios, Damian Ward, Kristen Balouch, Jeremy Tugeau, and Michele Noiset

O is for Old School: A Hip Hop Alphabet for B.I.G. Kids Who Used to be Dope by James Tyler and Ella Cohen

Raised on Hip-Hop by Jessica Chiha and Alex Lehours

The Roots of Rap: 16 Bars on the 4 Pillars of Hip-Hop by Carole Boston Weatherford and Frank Morrison

When the Beat Was Born: DJ Kool Herc and the Creation of Hip Hop by Laban Carrick Hill and Theodore Taylor III

Index

ENJOY THE REST OF THE CHILD'S INTRODUCTION SERIES!

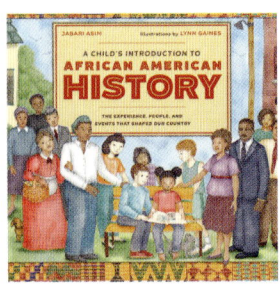

A Child's Introduction to African American History

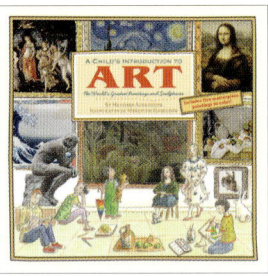

A Child's Introduction to Art

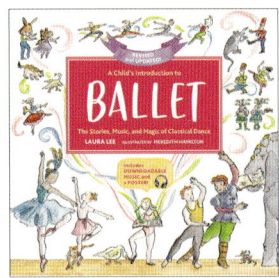

A Child's Introduction to Ballet

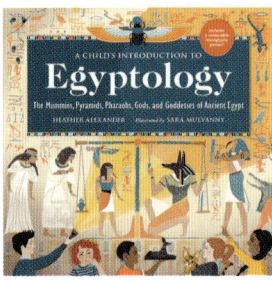

A Child's Introduction to Egyptology

A Child's Introduction to the Environment

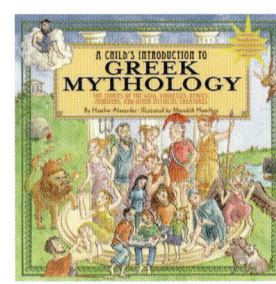

A Child's Introduction to Greek Mythology

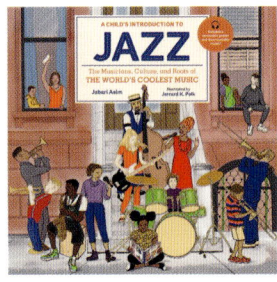

A Child's Introduction to Jazz

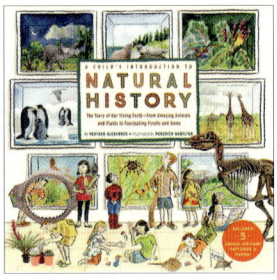

A Child's Introduction to Natural History

A Child's Introduction to the Night Sky

A Child's Introduction to Norse Mythology

A Child's Introduction to the Nutcracker

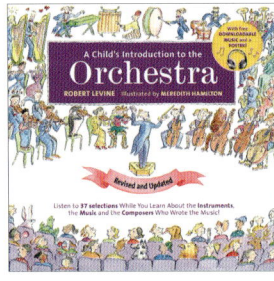

A Child's Introduction to the Orchestra

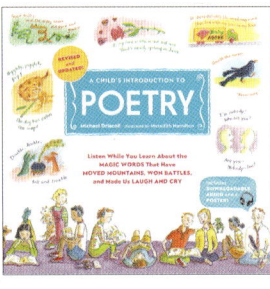

A Child's Introduction to Poetry

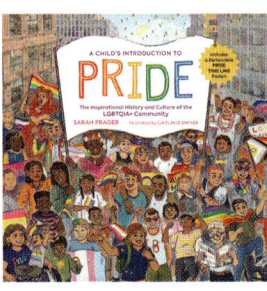

A Child's Introduction to Pride

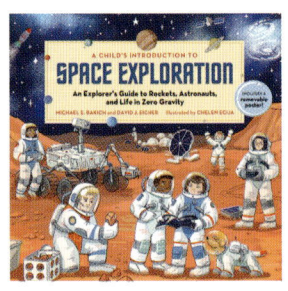

A Child's Introduction to Space Exploration

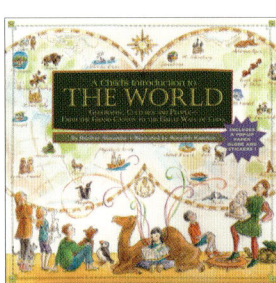

A Child's Introduction to the World

BLACK DOG
& LEVENTHAL
PUBLISHERS